Thy Hidden Ones

Union with Christ
Traced in the
Song of Songs

THY HIDDEN ONES

Union with Christ
Traced in the
Song of Songs

Jessie Penn-Lewis

CLC ✦ Publications

Fort Washington, Pennsylvania 19034

Published by CLC ❖ Publications

U.S.A.
P.O. Box 1449, Fort Washington, PA 19034

GREAT BRITAIN
51 The Dean, Alresford, Hants. SO24 9BJ

AUSTRALIA
P.O. Box 419M, Manunda, QLD 4879

NEW ZEALAND
10 MacArthur Street, Feilding

Originally published by
The Overcomer Literature Trust
England

This American Edition 1995

ISBN 0-87508-735-3

*Scripture quotations are generally from the English
Revised Version of 1881, which is similar to the
American Standard Version of 1901.*

This printing 2002

Printed in the United States of America

PREFACE

The "Song of Songs" is the very last portion of the sacred Scriptures that I would personally have chosen to write upon, but during a period of enforced rest it was so illuminated to me as the heart-history of a soul in its progress in the divine life that I was constrained to write; and as I did so, the conviction grew that I dared not withhold the light given.

The language of the "Song" must be read as pertaining to the spiritual realm alone; and there is no book in the Bible requiring more reverent reading, greater freedom from all earthly sentiment, and deeper recollectedness of the majesty of the High and Holy One who inhabits eternity.

It is often described as a love song between Christ and His Church, but it is also a mirror upon which the Divine Spirit flashes photographs, so to speak, of the glorified Lord, first from one standpoint and then from another, so that beholding as in a mirror the glory of the Lord, the soul may be transfigured into the same image, from glory to glory.

If read as the personal progress of the soul along the path of life, it accords with the key notes of all Scripture: death and resurrection. The passages usually interpreted as describing retrogression through worldliness have doubtless been used by the Holy Spirit to restore those who have left their first love. However, there is also a deeper meaning for those who are pressing on to know God and are not conscious of any "backsliding"—ones who yet know by personal experience the "wildernesses" of life, and from which they are to emerge to a fuller life in God.

It is far from my thoughts to stereotype "experiences," or to present the life of God in any systematized form. I desire simply to interpret those parts of Canticles which throw light upon the inworking of the Divine Spirit. I have therefore not attempted a full exposition of the text, but have rather confined myself to tracing the inner heart-history of the soul who is brought into personal union with Christ.

Moreover, this book will not meet the needs of those who desire directions as to the practical application of the Ten Commandments or the twelfth chapter of Romans; but others, who long to know the hidden life as the *spring* of practical duty, may find herein their portion of meat in due season.

I can only ask my readers to put the book aside if it contains no personal message to themselves, and to seek, direct from God, that union with the Well-Beloved which it describes.

It only remains to add that, with a few exceptions, I have omitted all historical and prophetical teaching, all explanations of the figurative setting of the "Song"—in fact, all the details that may be found in a commentary. The references are taken from the Revised Version, except where otherwise marked. Quotations from Conybeare and Howson's translation of the Epistles of St. Paul are indicated by the letters "CH."

May the Eternal Spirit Himself guard the language which expresses so faintly the most sacred things of God, and may He keep it from becoming mere phraseology on the lips of any who are seeking to enter into all His purposes. "Whereunto we have already attained," may each one manifest the broken spirit, the deep humility, the godly awe that bears such unmistakable witness to the "Practice of the Presence of God."

Jessie Penn-Lewis
May 1899

"Thou hidden Life of faithful souls—Thou Light
  Of that mysterious world of inner thought,
Oh give us grace to follow Thee aright,
  From cross and toil and sorrow shrinking not;
    Content to be but little known.
    Content to wander on alone;
    Here—hidden inwardly in Thee;
    There—Light in Thine own Light to be."

CONTENTS

Section IV

Section V

Section VI

Chapter 1

"Ye are My friends, if ye do the things which I command you" (John 15:14).

THE SONG OF SONGS

"The Song of Songs, which is Solomon's" (1:1).

Solomon prefigured the crowned Conqueror of Calvary, the risen and ascended Jesus, when He had by Himself purged our sins and "sat down on the right hand of the Majesty on high" (Hebrews 1:3). It is important to remember that He is now the Glorified One, that He has completed His work of redemption, that He has sat down a triumphant Conqueror, that He is now a waiting, expectant Lord—this one who gave His life to redeem out of the earth, from among fallen sinners, a Bride to share His Throne, lifting up a "beggar from the dunghill" to "inherit the throne of glory" (1 Samuel 2:8, KJV).

It is essentially the song "which is *Solomon's*,"

because it is the Song of the Heavenly Bridgroom over each soul who is a member of His purchased Bride; and it is a song shared in by the purchased one, because it is His song in her, as she is brought into heart union with her Lord—for all in her is of Him, through the Holy Spirit.

The song of the Bridegroom finds an echo in every bridal soul. "No man could learn the song" save they that had been "purchased out of the earth" (Revelation 14:3). It is a song to be sung through eternity. In the Song of Songs we have unveiled to us the heart history of the redeemed one who is led on to know the Lord. Veiled in language to be understood alone by the teaching of the Eternal Spirit, we see how the Heavenly Bridegroom woos the soul for whom He died, leads it on from one degree of union to another, draws it with the cords of His love to forsake itself and its own life, and then causes it to know in real experience one life with Him "who was declared to be the Son of God with power . . . by the resurrection of the dead" (Romans 1:4).

In the first chapters of the Song the Bridegroom simply calls His purchased one His *friend* (1:9, 15, mg.), His "companion" (KJV, mg.), or, as it is in the text, His "love."He describes her as the "fairest among women" (1:8), calls her His dove be-

---

Note: "mg"="margin." This indicates a marginal, alternative translation.

cause of the presence of the Holy Spirit in her, but not yet His *bride*.

This marks the earliest stage of the surrendered life; for friendship with Christ means obedience to His will and loyalty to His interests—an intercourse very precious, but far removed from the union that He desires. "Ye are My friends, if ye *do* . . ." (John 15:14). "I have called you friends; for all things that I heard from My Father I have made known unto you" (John 15:15). These words speak of a stage of fellowship beyond that of a servant, but far short of that of a bride.

The Soul's Cry After God

"Let Him kiss me with the kisses of His mouth" (1:2).

The soul is already a purchased one; she has heard the Saviour say, "Thou art *Mine*." She has answered, "I am Thine," and has found peace through the blood of the cross. It may be that she has remained at this point many years, knowing nothing of her Redeemer as the Bridegroom of her soul. But the heavenly vision has come! Somehow, somewhere, by the grace of God, she has had the revelation of a life of union with Christ that stirs her heart to intense desire. By the inworking of the Divine Spirit, she is moved to ask for the fullest knowledge of her God that is possible.

"Let Him kiss me!" she cries. She has known

the Father's kiss of reconciliation when she fled to His feet as a prodigal child. But this is more. This is the cry of the soul for the most intimate communion and fellowship with the Father and the Son that is conceivable.

It is the cry of the bride-spirit, drawn forth by God Himself, "for whom He foreknew, He also foreordained to be conformed to the image of His Son" (Romans 8:29), "even as He chose us in Him before the foundation of the world, that we should be holy and without blemish before Him in love" (Ephesians 1:4).

The soul must always have a heavenly vision to draw it out of itself and away from the things of earth. The "eyes of the heart" must be illumined to know the hope of its calling. The clearer the vision, the more entire the dependence upon the Holy Spirit for its fulfillment and the more intense the thirst after God—a "furnace of intense desire" which must be created by the Eternal Spirit Himself, and which is the supreme condition for knowing God.

The Soul's Vision

"Thy love is better than wine" (1:2).

We shall prove ourselves to be little worthy of the heavenly calling if we think alone of what we "give up." "Thy love is *better*," exclaims this soul in the Song of Songs. We lose only the dross when we exchange the earthly treasures for the heavenly ones. All that is of earth lasts but for a moment, but God satisfies forever.

The Soul's Choice

> "Thy Name is as ointment poured forth; therefore do the virgins* love Thee. Draw me; we will run after Thee"(1:3–4).

It is the "Name," as representing the Person of the Lord, which always attracts the soul—for our hearts need a Person. "Thy Name is as ointment poured forth; *therefore* do the virgins love Thee." The young ones have been won by Him, and they love Him at first for all the joy He gives them; they love the Giver for His gifts. But the soul who has had the heavenly vision cries, "Draw me, we will run after *Thee*." "That I may know *Him*" is the cry awakened by the Divine Spirit.

Moreover, as the purchased one follows on to know the Lord, these "virgins" will be drawn too. Unless we press on to full growth in the spiritual life, we stand in the way of others; but we unconsciously exercise an attractive force towards God if we seek to know Him fully and to walk with Him.

---

* *Almah*, the Hebrew word translated "virgin" here, is derived from the root word *awlam*, meaning "to veil from sight." In that sense, virgins are "hidden ones"—as spoken of throughout this book.

The surrendered soul knows, too, that the work is His, and that He, by His Spirit, must draw her out of herself into Him as her abiding place. "We *will* run after Thee," she says. Her part is in the will alone; she can but abandon herself to the skillfulness of His hands and respond to His drawing.

The King's Chambers

> "Draw me; we will run after Thee. The King hath brought me into His chambers. We will be glad and rejoice in Thee; we will make mention of Thy love. . . . In uprightness do they love Thee" (1:4, mg.).

The soul has no sooner been brought to a deliberate choice of God alone than she exclaims, "The King hath brought me into His chambers." Not the "banqueting house," be it noted, but "chambers"—where she will be prepared for fuller knowledge of her Lord. This, in the experience of the purchased one, may be the revelation of the Comforter—the Holy Spirit of promise. He has already imparted to her the gift of eternal life, and all her desires after God are inbreathed by Him, but she has never recognized Him as a Person—as the One given by the Father to take of the things of Jesus and show them unto her. She has therefore been disposed to place too much importance upon *her* consecration, or faith, rather than upon Him and His inworking. She has therefore not had the comfort of knowing Him to be dwelling in her as a personal Teacher, charged by the Father and the Son to lead her into all the fullness of God.

"The King hath brought me in. . . . We will be glad . . . ; we will make mention of Thy love!" exclaims the soul. Through the fresh revelation of God to the surrendered one, the young "virgins" learn to rejoice in the Well-Beloved rather than in His gifts, so that they too see His glory and speak of Him. When they converse one with another it will not now always be of "Christian work," but, leaving the work to the day when it will be tested by fire, they speak of His love. This joyous, spontaneous speaking of the person of Christ is only possible when walking with Him in "uprightness" (margin), with "a conscience void of offense toward God and man."

O Christ, the Anointed One, "rightly do they love Thee."

The Revelations in the King's Chambers

> "I am black, but comely, O ye daughters of Jerusalem, as the tents of Kedar, as the curtains of Solomon" (1:5).

The "terrible crystal" (Ezekiel 1:22) of the manifested presence of God the Holy Spirit reveals all that is of earth as blackness indeed. "I am black," cries the soul who has been brought into the light of God.

Not "black" with deliberate disobedience and

sin, for the purchased one, in seeking to know her God, must have put aside all that was knowingly wrong in her life so as to have been brought into the King's chambers.

The Spirit of God deals deeply with all who truly say, "We *will* run after Thee," as He reveals all that is contrary to the mind of God in heart and life. If the soul is obedient at every point, then the moment comes when the light breaks in and in the King's chambers the redeemed one cries, "I am black!" Not now begrimed with the sins that have been put away and cleansed in the precious blood of Christ, but black *in herself*, in her creature-life, in all her accursed inheritance from the first Adam. Once she only thought of the blackness of *sin*; now she sees that her comeliness as a creature is corruption (see Daniel 10:8), and her language is "Mine eye seeth Thee. Wherefore I abhor *myself*" (Job 42:5–6, KJV).*

When this self-abhorrence is real and deep, the soul has no hesitation in acknowledging it. Many desire the "self-life" to be dealt with in *secret* and are not willing to be as honest before others as they are before God; but this pride must be broken ere deliverance comes. All "keeping up" of even *spiritually religious* "appearances" must be surrendered, so that we may be brought into a life of

---

* See Appendix, Note A.

transparent reality before both God and man.

"I am black, but comely, O ye daughters," cries the purchased one. "Black in myself as the rough, unsightly tents of Kedar, but comely as the beautiful curtains of Solomon." She turns to the finished work of her Redeemer, knowing that she is "accepted in the Beloved," and covered with His comeliness in the eyes of a Holy God.

> One with Him, O Lord, before Thee,
>   There I live, and yet not I;
> Christ it is who there adores Thee;
>   Who more dear, or who more nigh?
> All the Father's heart mine own—
> Mine—and yet His Son's alone.
>
> *W.R.*

Chapter 2

"If any man cometh unto Me, and hateth not . . . his own life . . . , he cannot be My disciple" (Luke 14:26).

THE SOUL'S
SELF-KNOWLEDGE

"Look not upon me . . . because the sun hath scorched me. My mother's sons were incensed against me, *they* made me keeper of the vineyards; but mine own vineyard have I not kept" (1:6).

The purchased one has been an active worker, a "keeper of vineyards," appointed by others. In the light of God she discovers this, as well as the fruitlessness of work that is the outcome of "creaturely activity." She has thought more of service than of conformity to the image of Christ. Like Martha, she has been "distracted about much serving" (Luke 10:40, mg.), and, in caring for the needs of others, she has failed to sit at His feet to hear His word.

The soul now begins to feel the pain of being

misunderstood and misjudged by other children of God. They had thought her a most consecrated worker, and cannot understand her bitter self-reproach and her cry that she is "black." Did she not walk in victory? Was she not used of God? Then what does this sudden exclamation mean? They did not know how she had suffered in secret under the increasing conviction of utter failure. They had not seen what was passing between her and her God. It was true that she had laid aside every weight and had walked in victory up to the light she had, but now—all that she had thought beautiful looked black, and all her "consecrated" activity nought but a hideous, loathsome self. "Look not upon me," she cries, "because the sun hath *scorched* me!" "God is a Sun, a consuming fire—He has scorched me with His terrible holiness: woe is me, for I am undone; I have seen the King" (Isaiah 6:5).

The soul is so conscious of what she is in herself that she feels as if she had been laid bare to every human eye, as well as to the eye of God, and all praise or esteem from those around her becomes most painful. All desire to be "looked up to," or honored, passes away. She only craves a deeper abasement so that her Lord alone may be seen.

The Soul's Cry to the Well-Beloved

> " Tell me, O Thou whom my soul loveth, where Thou feedest
> Thy flock, where Thou makest it to rest at noon: for why
> should I be as one that wandereth?" (1:7, mg.).

She turns away from the misjudgments of other Christians and the bitter self-knowledge that has broken in upon her and turns to the Beloved of her soul. *He* at least will understand. *He* knows how her heart's cry is after Himself, that she has chosen to count all things loss for the excellency of the knowledge of Christ Jesus her Lord. *He* knows how she loathes herself, and how she rests as never before upon His righteousness as her only merit before the throne of God. He knows, He loves, He cares! She turns to Him with the cry of her whole being. "*Tell* me," she exclaims, "tell me, where Thou makest Thy flock to rest at noon!"

The beginning of the new life is likened to day-break, and its maturity to the noontide, free from all mists and shadows. "The path of the righteous is as the light of dawn, that shineth more and more unto the perfect day" (Proverbs 4:18, mg.). "Thy life shall arise above the noonday; though there be darkness, it shall be as the morning" (Job 11:17, mg.).

It is the purpose of God that each new-born soul should be led on, past the shadows, into the full clear light of life in the Holiest of All; yet how many abide in the twilight and never emerge into that "rest at noon" which pictures the rest in the heart of God in union with the Only Begotten of the Father.

"Tell me about that noontide rest," cries the surrendered one, for she fears lest she should lose the vision He has given her. In the midst of all the strife of tongues on the part of those who once made her a keeper of the vineyards, she fears lest she should be turned from her fixity of purpose and become as one tossed to and fro, "one that wandereth"—an *aimless* soul—beside the flocks of His companions.

The Well-Beloved's Instructions

> "If thou know not, O thou fairest among women, go thy way forth by the footsteps of the flock, and feed thy kids beside the shepherds' tents" (1:8).

The Well-Beloved immediately responds to the heartcry of the soul with the words, "*If* thou know not," revealing that, in some measure, she is responsible for her ignorance. Her directions are written in the Book, but her eyes have been restrained from knowing Him as One with the Father and as the door to the Father's heart.

He feeds His flock at "noon" within the sanctuary, and did they but know the Great Shepherd of the sheep and the power of the blood of the eternal covenant (Hebrews 13:20), they would go in and out and find pasture from the moment they became His sheep.

Although the "rest at noon" describes a maturity of experience, only realized in its fullness as the soul presses on to know its God, yet from the very beginning of the spiritual life the believer is "accepted in the Beloved." Each child of God, at every stage of growth, may have *boldness* to enter the Holiest by the blood of Jesus and is bidden to draw near with a true heart in full assurance of faith, having the heart sprinkled from an evil conscience (Hebrews 10:19, 22), with a certainty of finding grace to help in time of need.

The Well-Beloved calls the soul the "fairest among women" in spite of her description of herself as black; for the blacker she is in her own eyes, the fairer she is in His.

> "Oh soul, I will show thee the wonder,
>   The worth of My priceless blood;
> Thou art whiter than snow on the mountains,
>   Thou art fair in the eyes of God."

In answer to her desire for instruction, He directs her to go forth in the footsteps of the flock and to continue her work quietly beside the shepherds' tents.

When the surrendered one finds that other devoted children of God apparently fail to understand her path, or to comprehend the heavenly vision which draws her on to an obedience to Him they perhaps think unnecessary, there is the danger that she should forsake the "assembling together" (Hebrews 10:25) in the shepherds' tents, or cease to see the necessity of continuing faithful to that which is least in the Master's service, and any special responsibility that has been committed to her hand.

In the Holy Spirit's leading of the soul through the stripping of what may be called "consecrated self," and its activity, it is most important that there should be a faithful fulfillment of all outward "duty," that the believer may learn to act on *principle* rather than on pleasant impulse.

"Go thy way forth by the footsteps of the flock," is the Well-Beloved's instruction to His purchased one. Not "shut thyself away with the few who understand thee," but go forth in the path of duty, and leave to the faithful Lord the time and the way in which your petition shall be fulfilled, and you shall know the "rest at noon" in the heart of God.

Nevertheless, O soul, as you do go forth with the flock, under the Great Shepherd's tender leading, take heed lest you are more concerned to keep step with the flock than with your Beloved, for you must have your eyes on Him alone, and then He will lead you forth, by the right way, to the city of habitation.

Chapter 3

"*He that hath My commandments, and keepeth them, he it is that loveth Me; . . . and I will . . . manifest Myself unto him*" (John 14:21).

THE KING'S VOICE

"I have compared thee, O My friend, to the steeds in Pharaoh's chariots" (1:9, mg.).

In answer to her cry, the King Himself speaks to her in words of cheer. She recognizes His voice, even as a babe knows its mother's voice, because the divine life implanted in the blood-bought soul responds intuitively to the voice of its Creator.

In this first degree of union with the Lord He seems to speak little and seldom. The "pouring out" is on the side of the one seeking to know Him. He answers her briefly, and encourages her with the renewal of His promises. Unbroken communion with Him is not yet established.

Her heart's cry is "My soul followeth *hard* after

Thee" (Psalm 63:8), reminding us of the words of the Lord Jesus, "The Kingdom of heaven is gotten by force" (Matthew 11:12, mg.), or, as the original suggests, "*Those who have a vehement desire seize upon it.*" This intense, vehement pressing on to know the Lord,* and the consequent abandonment to the Holy Spirit for His work to be done at any cost, is what the Well-Beloved now beholds in His friend, and what He compares to the swift course and quick obedience of the beautiful steeds harnessed to the royal chariot of Pharaoh. It has been said that it is unnecessary to drive a soul that goes without driving! When once the will is wholly surrendered to God, and the decision made to obey and follow at all costs, the Spirit is able very rapidly to do His work. It is our delay and ceaseless controversy that grieves and hinders the Lord, and ever keeps back the child of God from emerging out of the region of strife into deepest rest.

The King's Promises

" Thy cheeks are comely with plaits of hair. . . . WE† will make thee plaits of gold with studs of silver" (1:10–11).

The Well-Beloved sees much natural comeliness in this seeking soul, much of her own life and strength, which the "plaits of hair" seem to sig-

---

* See Appendix, Note B.
† "The Trinity, implied by the Holy Spirit, whether it was so by the writer of the Song or not."—Fausset.

nify—much that might be called beautiful from our earthly point of view. But He promises, by the skillful workmanship of the triune God, that the life of earth shall give place to that divine life of which gold is always a type. "Plaits of gold" imply much fire, for gold is only workable when melted.

Nevertheless "We will" do it, says the Well-Beloved. The triune God undertakes the work—a work that can only be done in fallen sinners upon the basis of redemption. The gold shall have studs of silver—silver typifying the redemption of Calvary.

The promise of the Bridegroom may also be taken as the promise to His purchased one of the *"crown"*—"borders of gold with studs of silver" (KJV)—when the heavenly Bride will reign with Him, for the word "spouse," in Hebrew, means a "crowned one."*

The surrendered soul, pressing on for the prize of the high calling of God in Christ Jesus, is promised, on the word of the triune God, that the work shall be done. She shall know the divine life in union with the Glorified One; she shall sit down with Him in His throne and be a partaker of His glory.

O longing heart, your God has promised to ful-

---

* Fausset.

fill all your desire. Rest upon His royal Word in all that is to come. The word of the Lord may try you, as it did His servant Joseph, but *it came to pass* then, and it shall be fulfilled to you.

You have sought to know one life with your Lord. The promise is yours, "WE WILL."

"Hath He said, and shall He not do it? or hath He spoken, and shall He not make it good?" (Numbers 23:19). You shall say in His time, in deep humility:

"One life alone between us now,
    One life—the life *Thou* livest."

The King's Table

> "While the King sat at His table, my spikenard sent forth its fragrance. My Beloved is unto me as a bundle of myrrh, that lieth betwixt my breasts" (1:12–13).

The voice of the Lord restores the calm and brings back to the troubled one the knowledge that the King is sitting at His table within her heart.

She had become occupied with self-revelation—the immediate result of her entrance into the King's chambers and the consequent misjudgments of her "mother's sons." The strife of tongues had made her fear lest she should mistake the path, and in agony of soul she had turned to Him. Would *He* not tell her what to do; will *He* let her go astray? Her very helplessness is her safety, for she knows she must depend upon Him if she is to walk upon that path "where fools shall not err" (Isaiah 35:8).

In answer to her cry, the Well-Beloved speaks and comforts her, telling her that He has undertaken the whole matter and reminding her of His presence, so that again she rests upon His faithfulness and retires within, away from all the exterior tumult, to blessed communion with her Lord. "When He giveth quietness, who then can make trouble?" (Job 34:29, KJV). In fellowship with Him, her spikenard (the emblem of humility—a grace only possible through His divine indwelling) sends forth its fragrance, and He fulfills His promise:

> "If any man . . . open the door, I will come in to him, and will sup with him, and he with Me" (Revelation 3:20).

At His table the Well-Beloved opens His heart to His redeemed one, even as He did the night before His crucifixion to the little band who followed Him all the way to Calvary.

"These things I said not unto you at the *beginning*," He stated (John 16:4, KJV). The Beloved has much to say to His own which cannot be said "at the beginning." He must first say, "Follow Me," and draw us away from other interests and other possessions, before He can tell us of a path that is "expedient" for us, one leading to fuller knowledge of Himself. In closest communion at the

King's table the soul now learns from the lips of the Lord that if she is to know Him fully, she must expect suffering and sacrifice. Hitherto she has only had glimpses of the heavenly vision of Christ in His *glory*, which led her to cry, "Draw me; we will run after Thee." Now He asks her if she will follow Him even though it may mean the *cross*— as if He said to her as He did to His disciples, "Are ye able to drink the cup that I drink? or to be baptized with the baptism that I am baptized with?" (Mark 10:38).

Will she turn back?

It is one thing to respond to the Saviour's call; to have the heavenly vision of the glorified Lord; to willingly surrender the gifts for the Giver. But it is quite another to set our faces like a flint to go to Jerusalem after we have seen a little of what the true following of Christ will mean!

The decision *must* be made, and made so definitely that whatever comes we shall never shrink back. The bridge must be burned behind us, so to speak, so that there never can be a question of retreat.

The surrendered one sees that the Well-Beloved must first be a Bridegroom of bitterness, a "bundle of myrrh," before she can know Him in His glory. She reveals the true bride-spirit and proves her heavenly calling by asking no better lot than befell her Lord. She consents to follow Him at all costs; she clasps the myrrh to her breast and exclaims: "My Beloved is unto *me* as a bundle of myrrh," yea, even as "a cluster of *cypress*" (1:14, KJV, mg.). Myrrh, costly and bitter, is obtained only through the knife's incision in the tree! Cypress, the funeral or cemetery tree of the East, is the tree that signifies death!

O soul, what can you say to the King at His table? What can you say to Him with the pierced hands but, "I will not leave Thee" (2 Kings 2:6)? "My heart is fixed, O God, my heart is fixed" (Psalm 57:7).

> Behold, My bride, how fair My mouth, Mine eyes;
> My heart is glowing fire, My hand is grace—
> And see how swift My foot, and follow Me.
> For thou with Me shalt scorned and martyred be,
> Betrayed by envy, tempted in the wilds.
>
> •   •   •
>
> And love shall wound, and steadfastness shall slay,
>   Yet thou shalt love Me still.
> The spear shall pierce thy heart; *My* life shall be
> The life that lives and moves henceforth in thee.
> Then, as a conqueror loosened from the cross,
> Thou shalt awaken and be borne above
> Upon the breath of Mine Almighty love.
>
> *(Mechthild of Hellfde, 1277)*

Chapter 4

"The Master saith, Where is My guestchamber, where I shall eat . . . with My disciples?" (Mark 14:14).

THE BANQUETING HOUSE

The Whisper of the King

"Behold, thou art fair, My friend; . . . thine eyes are as doves" (1:15).

The Well-Beloved beholds the Holy Dove, the Eternal Spirit of the Father, through whom He offered Himself unto God and became obedient unto death, "yea, the death of the cross," shining through the eye of the soul whose gaze is turned wholly toward Him in entire abandonment and trust.

Through the power of the same Spirit she has been enabled to yield herself wholly to her Lord, and she is becoming single-eyed in her choice of Christ and His cross at all costs. Therefore He exclaims, "Thou art fair, My friend; thou hast doves' eyes."

The Response of the Soul

> " Behold, *Thou* art fair, my Beloved. . . . *Our* couch is green.
> The beams of *our* house are cedars . . . *our* rafters are cy-
> presses. I am . . . a lily of the valleys"* (1:16–17, mg., and
> 2:1).

The soul in true self-effacement returns all the
praise to her Beloved, for she knows that she is
"fair" only through the indwelling presence of
her Lord. By His grace alone has her heart been
set to know Him and her will bent to choose to
follow Him fully. His people are "willing in the
day of [His] power" (Psalm 110:3, KJV). It is all of
grace.

She is getting to know her Well-Beloved better, and ventures to say "*our* house" and "*our*
rafters"; Thee and me. "All things are yours . . .
and ye are Christ's; and Christ is God's" (1
Corinthians 3:21–23). Her reference to the *cypress*
tree shows that she understands now, however
dimly, that union with Christ in His life is based
upon fellowship with Him in His death, for the
cypress grows in the necropolis, the "city of the
dead." Death and life are always linked together
in the teaching of Scripture—death to the old,

---

* It is generally assumed that the Bridegroom speaks here
and calls Himself the lily of the valleys, but the division in
the Revised Version does not support this. The words ac-
cord more with the response of the soul. "The Bride thus
speaks of herself as lowly though lovely, in contrast with the
apple tree, the Bridegroom."—Fausset.

accursed life and resurrection to the new is the one underlying principle throughout, whether given in plain or figurative language. "*Thou* art fair, my Beloved . . . but I—I am only a lily of the valleys!" Thus the soul responds to her Lord, saying in effect, "I am but a simple little flower, not worth Thy notice."

The King's Estimate of His Friend

> "As a lily among thorns, so is My friend among the daughters" (2:2, mg.).

"If you are a simple lily," says the Well-Beloved, "you are to My eyes as a lily among thorns." He sees His own life already growing up in her—with the selfsame features of humility and meekness— while He beholds others as still dwelling in the thorny life of earth. The earth-life can produce nothing else than thorns, "whose end is to be burned" (Hebrews 6:8). His "friend," who is fair to Him, is as a lily in their midst.

The Soul's Estimate of Her Well-Beloved

> "As the apple tree among the trees of the wood, so is my Beloved among the sons. I sat down under His shadow, . . . His fruit was sweet to my taste" (2:3).

She compares Him to a fruitful tree, and to her great delight finds in Him all she needs. She has been learning to say "our," and to find all things are hers in Christ; now she discovers that He is becoming all in all to her.

Once she said, "I am of Paul," or "I am of Apollos," as she gloried in men; but now she is losing sight of all the "sons" as she beholds the glory of Him who is the First-begotten from the dead. She is finding Him to be a shadow from the heat, a refuge from the storm, and, satisfied with Him alone, she sits down in perfect rest, finding His fruit sweet to her taste.

The Banqueting House

> "He brought me to the banqueting house, and His banner over me was love" (2:4).

As the Well-Beloved fills her vision and becomes all in all to her, she finds herself brought in by Him to the banqueting house, where in an overpowering revelation of His love He gives her a foretaste of the union which she seeks.

The spiritual manifestation of Christ in the heart is *love*. It has now pleased God to "reveal His Son" in her (Galatians 1:16). She had already had glimpses of this when she had fellowship with Him at His table, but now she has a revelation of Himself, and sees that wherever He may lead her henceforth, though it be along the way of the cross, it will be under the banner of love.

The soul is not able to bear the full answer to

all its desires. It cries to know all that oneness with the Risen Lord means to redeemed sinners, but it does not understand that it needs to be prepared and strengthened to endure it. "Stay me . . . for I am sick [with] love" (2:5), cries the surrendered one in the banqueting house. The revelation of Christ in His glory makes even an apostle fall at His feet as dead! (Revelation 1:17).

The soul asks for some support, for it all seems too much; but she remembers that *He is holding her* even while He reveals Himself to her, and she needs no other stay. "Underneath are the everlasting arms" (Deuteronomy 33:27). "His left hand is under my head, and His right hand doth embrace me" (2:6), she exclaims.

The Word of the King for Rest

> " I adjure you, O daughters of Jerusalem . . . that ye stir not up, nor awaken love, until it* please" (2:7).

The soul is now in retirement with her Beloved; she has entered into rest.

These "daughters" may typify other believers, true children of the Jerusalem which is above (Galatians 4:26), or else professors who know nothing of spiritual fellowship with the Lord—those

---

* "It" (RV) "He" (KJV) "She" (Septuagint) are three renderings given of this word! It seems more likely that the soul will be disturbed in *her* rest in Him, rather than that *He* who loves to the uttermost should be driven away.

who have a name to live and yet are dead. In either case, they form a group who are deeply concerned about this soul that is following on to know the Lord. They do not know how fully she is in His keeping, for He Himself has become the jealous keeper of His blood-bought one.

He sees the "daughters" ready to intrude. They will seek to "stir up" this soul, when the word of the King is for rest.

Since the hour she said "*Draw me;* we will run after Thee," He has tested her surrender and shown her more clearly the conditions of oneness with Him in His life. He has proved that she is steadfastly purposed to follow on to know the Lord. There is now a fixity of will that will enable Him to lead her on through deeper testings, without the delay of reasoning, rebellion, or hesitation.

But He will lead on softly. It is needful that she should be allowed some period for repose. "He knoweth our frame; He remembereth that we are dust" (Psalm 103:14). Resting upon His faithfulness, in the "assurance of understanding" (Colossians 2:2) that He now dwells in her heart as His settled place of abode, she will be strengthened in His own good time to hear His voice calling her to arise and follow on, so that she may be "filled unto all the fullness of God."

The Bridegroom speaks for her to the anxious

daughters, solemnly forbidding them to disturb her peace, as if He would say to her and them,

> "The Lord is in His holy temple: be silent before Him, all the earth" (Habakkuk 2:20, mg.).

> "God is in the midst of her; she shall not be moved" (Psalm 46:5).

"I charge *you*, O daughters, . . . that ye stir not up, nor awaken love until she please."

Chapter 5

"Blessed be God . . . who . . . begat us again . . . by the resurrection of Jesus Christ from the dead, unto an inheritance" (1 Peter 1:3–4).

THE CALL OF
THE RISEN CHRIST

"The voice of my Beloved! behold, He cometh, leaping upon the mountains" (2:8).

The soul resting in her Beloved suddenly hears His voice, and recognizes it at once. No other voice can move her now; others may tell her many things, but nothing pierces the inward ear until He speaks!

The Well-Beloved now manifests Himself to His purchased one as the Risen Lord. She sees Him coming toward her, leaping upon the mountains as a gazelle. His title in the margin of Psalm 22 is "the Hind of the morning"—a resurrection type. He seems to approach her as if He were away from her, without and not within her heart, tenderly alluring her into the wilderness to know her God. He has been revealed to her as dwelling in her heart, and we left her reveling in the joy of His presence in a blessed rest that no outward tumult could touch, no voice disturb.

Now she needs to be taught a trust in Himself alone, apart from His conscious revelations to her heart. Her faith must rest upon His character and His word, rather than upon His manifestations. She must care more for Him than for His vineyards; she must know that conformity to His likeness is more to Him than service.

The Attitude of the Risen Lord

> "My Beloved is like a gazelle. . . . Behold, He standeth behind our wall, He looketh in at the windows, He showeth Himself [or "glanceth," mg.] through the lattice" (2:9, mg.).

The Risen Lord approaches the soul from *without,* that He may draw her attention from her old experience *within.*

She sees that He is like a gazelle, rapid in movement, and that He is *standing,* no longer sitting at His table, but as if He were waiting for some response to His voice; "standing," she adds, "behind our wall!" She does not fear to say "our" now; she is growing bolder in her knowledge of Him, and is delighted to think that He is shut in with her in the banqueting house—in the inner retreat of her heart. She thinks this "wall" is of His planning, but she is mistaken; she does not know that it will hinder the manifestation of Him to others, and that it is part of the old earth-life that has to be dealt with later on.

There must come a "breaking down of the walls" (Isaiah 22:5), for there are no "walls" in the heavenly life. The Christ upon the cross of Calvary broke down the middle wall of partition between man and man, as well as between man and God (Ephesians 2:14–16). He died that in Him there might be a new creation, one new man, "perfected into *one*" (John 17:23). All divisions caused by sin cease in Him.

Oh soul, that "wall" that you are calling "*our* wall" must be broken down, if you are to be one with your Lord in His life of love poured out for others!

But the soul in the banqueting house is not thinking of "others"; she is too much absorbed in her days of heaven upon earth. She does not want to look over the "wall" at the broken hearts in this sorrow-stricken world. Like Peter, she would forget the multitude in the glory of the transfiguration mount.

Who is there that has known the coming of the Comforter, and the revelation of the Christ within, but will remember the temptation to spiritual self-esteem in those blessed days!

There was the danger of looking upon others with something of pity and unconscious *judgment*—of shrinking from duty for the luxury of retiring within for that inward communion with the Well-Beloved—of such absorption with Him that it was difficult to enter into the interests and affairs, apparently so trifling, of those around us—of incapacity to understand matters of really practical importance, because all outward things seemed only echoes of another world.

In the fuller light of the mountain vision, we see the imperfections of those days and understand why our "mother's sons were incensed against" us. They saw the possibility of spiritual selfishness and feared lest the *vineyards* should suffer.

They only failed in trusting the Lord that He who had begun the good work would surely finish it and would lead His redeemed one forth to more Spirit-energized activity in time to come.

The soul, rejoicing in the Well-Beloved's presence behind the "wall," fails to notice that His whole attitude expresses movement. He stands, as if ready to depart; He "looks in at the windows" of her soul; He flashes new rays of light; He "glances" through the lattice; He "shows Himself" to allure her to arise and follow—but she is too deeply satisfied with her "banqueting house" experience to understand. Later on, as she learns to know the Lord better, she becomes "quick of scent" in His will and intuitively detects the meaning of His movements; but now she is still too much in the heavy life of earth to understand anything less than plain language. He is obliged to speak *plainly*, and what is the message?

The Call of the Risen Lord

" My Beloved spake, and said unto me, Rise up, My friend, My fair one, and come away. . . . The winter is past; the rain is over. . . . The flowers appear . . . the time of pruning is come. . . . Arise, My friend . . . and come" (2:10–13, mg.).

The soul knows His voice, and knows that He speaks to her expressly. His language is plain: "*Rise up.*" What does He mean? He had brought her into rest, had forbidden others to disturb her, and now He says, "Come away!" Where to?

The time has come when she must be taught through personal experience her identification with the Lord in His death and her union with Him in His resurrection life, so that He may tell her "plainly of the Father" (John 16:25).

"I am the Way, . . . no one cometh unto the Father but by Me. . . . I go unto the Father. . . . Ye shall know that I am in My Father, and ye in Me, and I in you" (John 14:6, 12, 20), He said.

He died, the Just for the unjust, that He might

"*bring us to God*" (1 Peter 3:18, KJV). Through the rent veil of His flesh, He—the New and Living Way—seeks to lead us to abide with Him in the Father.

The Well-Beloved likens the past period of rest to winter, for inwardly the new life in her was being "rooted and grounded in love" (Ephesians 3:17), "to the end" that she might be strong to "apprehend," and be "filled unto all the fullness of God" (Ephesians 3:18–19). During the winter season, in nature, the sap goes downward to the roots, and all outward manifestation of life seems checked.

The Well-Beloved calls the soul to arise, because the winter is past; it is now becoming springtime, and the rain of the Spirit has been silently falling and preparing her for His fresh call. He sees the flowers appearing, and a luxuriant growth of waste wood that will need His careful pruning. He begins to deal more definitely with the outward "manner of life," so as to make it correspond with His inward possession of the heart. He has been doing a deep, silent work in her time of repose. *She*, appropriately, has been occupied with Him. *He* has been drawing forth strong roots into Himself, that she may be the better able to endure the pruning knife in its time.

"Arise, My friend, and come. You must cooperate with Me in all My working; you must work *out* all that I work *in,* if you are to know Me and the fullest power of My endless life. Come away, and I will lead you to know the Father." So speaks the Risen Lord.*

---

* See Appendix, Note C.

Chapter 6

"All we who were baptized unto Christ Jesus were baptized into His death" (Romans 6:3).

THE CLEFTS OF THE ROCK

"O My dove, that art in the clefts of the rock, . . . let Me see thy countenance, let Me hear thy voice; for sweet is thy voice, and thy countenance is comely" (2:14).

Wherever we turn in Scripture we find the story of the cross set forth, in many and different types and figures. Jesus Christ, smitten by God for us, is clearly set forth in the rock smitten by Moses in the wilderness (Exodus 17:6). We understand, also, the reference to the crucified Lord in the word of Jehovah to Moses when He said, "I will put thee in a cleft of the rock, and will cover thee with My hand until I have passed by" (Exodus 33:22).

We easily recognize the same underlying reference to the Crucified One—that "Rock of Ages cleft for me"—as we listen to the voice of the Risen Lord speaking to His redeemed one. He would turn her eyes to Calvary and teach her that she is hidden in His wounded side, planted by the Holy Spirit into His death (Romans 6:5).

Hitherto she has known Him as her indwelling King. She has had glimpses of the cross, and has agreed to follow Him in the pathway of the cross; but she has not yet fully apprehended her position as buried with Him by baptism into His death, and therefore separated from herself and from all the old life and its claims. She must know that the cross stands between her and the world—that she has died in her Redeemer—to be joined to Him in His resurrection life and, in His ascension, to abide within the veil.*

The Well-Beloved reminds the soul of her place in the cleft of the Rock, because He can recognize her as His betrothed one nowhere else!

The bride for the first Adam was taken out of his side during his sleep; made of his own nature and presented to him by her Creator—a marvelous foreshadowing of the mystery of Christ and His Church!

All the redeemed ones, born of the first Adam and under the curse, were, in the foreknowledge of God, planted into the God-man, the Second

---

* See Appendix, Note D.

Adam, hanging upon the cross of Calvary, and becoming a curse for them. "We thus judge that One died for all, therefore all died" (2 Corinthians 5:14). Planted into Him, baptized into His death, there emerges a Bride, formed of many members, taken out of His side in the sleep of death, partaking of His divine nature and eventually to be presented unto Him to share His throne.

The Well-Beloved entreats the soul to turn her face toward Him, and to let Him hear her voice in glad response to His call. He sees that her eyes are in the wrong direction. He had drawn her *within* from all outward things by the strong power of His manifested presence at the center of her being; but now He desires her to turn toward Him as *not* in her heart—although He is there—but as in His *Father's* bosom.

Sweet is the voice of the blood-bought one to the Beloved Lord; lovely to Him is the gaze of the soul that turns towards Him as the sunflower to the sun. She is to be as the moon that is a faithful witness to the unseen orb of day.

The Soul's Preoccupied Reply

" Take [i.e., Catch] us the foxes, the little foxes, that spoil the vineyards. . . . My Beloved is mine, and I am His; He feedeth . . . among the lilies" (2:15–16).

She hears the Well-Beloved's voice, sees His

attitude, and hearkens to His call to arise, His command to forget the things that are behind. She listens to His message about the cross, to His call to turn her face toward Him, but—*she does not understand!* She is preoccupied. She evidently has her eyes upon the internal vine and its promise of fruit, and is getting concerned in the keeping of her vineyard. Thus easily the gaze is turned away from the person of the Lord.

In the King's chambers the soul discovered that she had been too much engrossed in active service, and had *neglected* her own vineyard. Now she goes to the other extreme and is so *occupied with her vineyard* as not to be able to understand her Beloved's call. She is fearing lest she should lose the blessed experience of His indwelling, and begins to dread lest the vines should be spoiled. She is frightened at some "little foxes" that are appearing—"little" manifestations of the old life which she thought had gone, and gone forever. If she had remained occupied with her Lord so as to quickly obey when He said "Rise up," *He* surely would see to the young fruit and deal with the little foxes—for the Beloved can only manifest His delivering and keeping power while we are walking in His will. "Little foxes" always tell the tale that somewhere we have failed to keep step with the Lord. We have missed His will or failed to understand His voice. We must quickly deal with God over these "little things," for they open the door to great ones if not dealt with at once.

Oh soul, be quick and wait upon your Lord; you must fly to the cleft of the Rock and hide in Him. You have failed to understand His message of the cross. You *are* in Him, upon His cross. Fly to the place called Calvary, and you shall see Him dealing with the foxes and culturing the budding vine.

It is not enough for you to rest upon your old experience and comfort yourself that your Beloved is yours, or that He is still in your heart feeding upon the lilies of His own planting within you. You will have to learn that you must *press on* and walk in His will in sensitive obedience if you are to *know* the Lord.

Chapter 7

"I will go and return to My place, till they acknowledge their offence, and seek My face: in their affliction they will seek Me earnestly" (Hosea 5:15).

THE VALLEY OF TROUBLE

"Until the day break, and the shadows flee away, turn, my Beloved, and be Thou like a gazelle . . . upon the mountains of separation" (2:17, mg.).

The soul failed to understand the Bridegroom's call to arise and follow Him, and so He hides His face. He knows that this will cause her to seek Him. He has called upon her to turn her face toward Him, and she answered by talking about the vines and the foxes. He tells her about the hiding place from herself in the cleft of the Rock, and she sinks back upon her old experience and says, "My Beloved *is mine!*" (v. 16). That *He* should see of the travail of His soul and be satisfied—this is not yet the supreme desire of her heart. She cannot yet give Him the fellowship He seeks. What He is to *her* is still her main thought.

The Risen Lord now hides Himself to see what silence will do. There would have been no need for this had she left the vines and foxes to His dealing and quickly obeyed His call.

If we left ourselves entirely in His hands, and responded to His voice without hesitation or self-reflection, or any watching of ourselves and our experiences, how quickly we would be led to dwell in the secret place of the Most High! His silence and the hiding of His face arrest her in her self-absorption. She is evidently conscious that there is a cloud, and she seems to know now that she is not yet so fully in union with Him as she thought. She is still in the "day-dawn" of the spiritual life, but yet the Bright and Morning Star has arisen in her heart to herald the coming day of her one life with Him—a day which will be "as the light of the morning, when the sun riseth, a morning without clouds" (2 Samuel 23:4).

In the shadow that has come upon her soul through the silence of Him whom her soul loveth, she prays that He will turn His face toward her— turn with gazelle-like rapidity as of old—turn upon these terrible "mountains of separation." The "mountain life" seems far from her now, and to her deep humiliation *He* appears to be alone on the mountain, and she in the valley of darkness. She says she will be content, "until the day dawn, and the shadows flee away," if He will only turn toward her and give her one look!

Does He answer her cry? No—

The Lord is silent in His love (Zephaniah 3:17, mg.).

The Seeking Soul and Her Decision

"By night on my bed I sought Him . . . but I found Him not. I said, *I will rise now*, . . . I will seek Him" (3:1–2).

An old writer suggestively calls this the "night of faith," and the "bed" is the place in the heart where the Lord is wont to rest. This is spiritually true, for the soul is now in the darkness of night. The shadows have deepened instead of fleeing away. She seeks her Lord in the old retreat within her heart, but she seems to find Him not. In her desolation she is roused to activity and earnest seeking. Hither and thither she goes, seeking for her Beloved. Like Job she says:

"Behold, I go forward, but He is not there; and backward, but I cannot perceive Him; on the left hand, . . . but I cannot behold Him. . . . He hideth Himself on the right hand, that I cannot see Him. . . . God hath made my heart faint. . . . I am not dismayed because of the darkness, nor because thick darkness covereth my face!" (Job 23:8–9, 16–17, mg.).

She is not dismayed because of the darkness but will seek Him with her whole heart. So intent is she on finding Him that all reserve is gone—*the "wall" is giving way!* She now cares not who in the city knows, so long as she finds Him. She will confess to others that He has withdrawn Himself from her; she will speak to the "watchmen" and ask them if they can help her (v. 3)! The suffering is too keen to attempt to "keep up appearances," or to attempt to keep up past experience by more vigorous testimony. She must be honest. What matters it what people think of *her!* She must find Him!

The Well-Beloved has succeeded in His purpose. He had called her to arise, but she did not obey. By hiding His face, He has aroused her from her lethargy; by His silence, He has drawn her to seek Him diligently; by prolonging His apparent absence, He has broken down the wall of reserve and drawn her out of herself.

He watched her looking for Him in the old retreat. He noted her desolation, but He gave no sign. He saw her rushing hither and thither, to this or that place, expecting to obtain "blessing" as of old; but He did not use the old instruments, or instruct the hitherto-much-loved "watchman" with an answer that met her need. He was silent in His love. It was because He desired to lead His loved one on to know Him fully that He allowed her thus to think Him gone. "He doth not afflict willingly, nor grieve the children of men" (Lamentations 3:33).

With joy He witnessed His end attained, and saw His redeemed one "rise up" to seek Him. How tenderly He noted her intensity of purpose, and her determination to find Him at the cost even of her reputation in the religious world.

He has but dealt with her as He did with the disciples on the lake, when in the storm "He would have passed by them" (Mark 6:48), so as to draw out their cry of need; or again at Emmaus, when "He made as though He would go further" (Luke 24:28), so that they might constrain Him to tarry with them.

The Seeking Soul's Reward

> "It was but a little that I passed from them, when I *found Him*. . . . I held Him, and would not let Him go" (3:4).

How small a step stands often between the soul and freedom! The failure of all things around throws it upon God in utter helplessness. Some great pressure of need, some "desperation point," and the soul is at liberty. For so long as we are able to maintain the outer "wall," cover our failures, hide our deepest feelings, and live in *secret* through all God's breakings, we can remain within the rigid limit of our narrow selves.

In Canticles it was the intense heartcry after the Well-Beloved that drew the soul out of itself, away from old experiences and all created means of blessing.

To "pass by" all is simply to part with all pre-conceived ideas of His working—all plan of time or place or instrument—to be still, and to leave to Him the way of blessing. To "come out of one's self" is to be so broken as to lose all thought of self—all self-interest, self-glory, self-complacency, self-appropriation. To rise and seek Him is but the pouring out at His feet of the yearning cry of the heart, the furnace of intense desire awakened by the Divine Spirit. The "vacuum" is ready for God to fill.

To "find Him" means that our earnest seeking has given place to quiet resting upon the statement of the Lord, "You are in the cleft of the Rock," and to the turning of the eyes of the heart toward Him as the living One.

In a transport of joy the purchased one says that she "found Him," and adds, "I held Him, and would not let Him go" (v. 4). His manifested presence is so precious that now she is disposed to watch and cling to it, lest she should lose it again.

Ah soul, it is not for *you* to retain *Him. To grasp is to lose in divine things.* He will abide if you will trust yourself to Him and learn to let Him go as He wills. It is not for you to watch and rest on His manifestations, but to trust Him and rely on His declaration alone. Nay, even more—He will not veil His presence when you pass from all thought of yourself to dwell in Him; when you yield up your own life to live by Him, as He lived by the Father.

Chapter 8

"Having been buried with Him . . . ye were also raised with Him through faith in the working of God, who raised Him from the dead" (Colossians 2:12).

THE POWER OF
HIS RESURRECTION

"I adjure you, O daughters of Jerusalem, . . . that ye stir not up, nor awaken love, until it please" (3:5).

The Risen Lord again forbids the "daughters" to touch a soul so entirely in His keeping. He knows what she has suffered in the anguish of His apparent withdrawal, and the agony of her self-reproach over the least unfaithfulness or self-absorption.

It has been well said that sins are relative. "The more a soul is favored, the greater the gifts entrusted to it, the closer its union with its Lord, . . . the greater is the sin of the very least and apparently most trifling unfaithfulness. An act which in a stranger would be nothing, in a trusted servant would be a crime."*

Others may be content with being kept from what is visibly and grossly *sin*, but the obedient heart, seeking to walk with Him in unbroken communion, cannot excuse the faintest disobedience or lack of sensitiveness to His will.

The tender Lord knows all this and again gives His loved one a time of rest, lest, as He says, "the spirit should faint away . . . before Me" (Isaiah 57:16, mg.).

The Well-Beloved knows, too, that His purchased one must be strengthened with might by the Spirit before He can lead her further. He again speaks to the eager daughters and bids them not disturb her rest, for He has allured her into the wilderness to speak comfortably to her. The valley of trouble will prove to be the door through which she will pass to a fuller union with her Lord. *There* He will betroth her unto Him in faithfulness, and she shall know the Lord. *There* she will learn to call Him "Ishi" instead of Baali, and she "shall sing there" (see Hosea 2:14–16, mg., 20).

Oh that the children of the Lord would allow Him to care for His own children! He who has redeemed each soul at such tremendous cost will deal with each one tenderly, according to its need

---

* *The Names of God*—Andrew Jukes.

and to its character. They are safe in His pierced hands. "A bruised reed shall He not break, and the dimly burning wick shall He not quench" (Isaiah 42:3, mg.).

The Transfigured Soul

> "Who is this that cometh up out of the wilderness like pillars of smoke, perfumed with myrrh and frankincense?" (3:6).*

After the period of retirement commanded by the Well-Beloved, the daughters see the betrothed one emerging from the wilderness, and they glorify God in her.

They had known of her sorrow; for did she not go about the city seeking the Lord? Did she not ask the watchmen to help her? Her friends exclaim, "Who is this?" What a change has taken place! She was then desolate, broken, weeping, but now she is a transfigured soul, and the days of her mourning are ended. She is coming up out of the wilderness with the glory of the Lord seen upon her, and they liken her to a "pillar of smoke." This expression is used by the prophet Joel in describing God's wonders in the days when He will pour out His Spirit in Pentecostal fullness upon His ser-

---

* It is not clear of whom this is spoken, but in the context it corresponds to the thought that the soul has been passing through a wilderness; so it seems to refer to her. In any case, if it refers to the King, she is united to Him and they are *one*.

vants and handmaidens (Joel 2:28–30). The God of glory also manifested His presence in a "pillar of cloud" (Exodus 13:22) when He went forth before His people Israel. From these references we may therefore gather that the soul emerges from the wilderness manifestly in the power of the Holy Spirit, and the "wall" that hid her indwelling Lord from others has been broken down.

It is worth going through the wilderness for this; worth the cost of the apparent forsaking by the Well-Beloved, to come forth perfumed with *myrrh*—with the fragrance that alone can come from fellowship with Him of whom it was written, "It pleased the Lord to bruise Him; He hath put Him to grief" (Isaiah 53:10). She is also a *melted* soul, no longer hard and unbending, but tender and broken with His love; so pliable and yielding to His will that she is compared to frankincense, a liquid distilled gum. The melting power of the love of God can now be manifested through her, so that others are broken at His feet.

The Victorious Soul

> "Behold, it is the litter of Solomon; threescore mighty men are about it. . . . All handle the sword and are expert in war. Every man hath his sword . . . because of fear in the night" (3:7–8).

The daughters exclaim, "Who is this?" and then they add, "Behold, it is the litter of Solomon!"

They see a triumphal procession emerging from the wilderness: the palanquin of the King guarded by mighty men equipped for war. Historically, this is said to refer to the Lord Jesus emerging from His conflict with the Adversary in the wilderness.

The soul united to the conqueror of Calvary shares in His triumph over principalities and powers, for at His cross He put them to open shame (Colossians 2:14–15). Abiding in the victorious Lord, she will be carried safely over all the pitfalls and wiles of the devil, for she is encompassed by angels of light, "mighty men," who are expert in war against the legions of darkness (see Revelation 12:7–11). These legions of darkness are "wicked spirits" who attack, always in the dark and suddenly, when the soul is passing through a "night" of trial.

The God-Possessed Soul

> "King Solomon made himself a palanquin of the wood of Lebanon, . . . the pillars thereof of silver, the bottom thereof of gold, the seat of it of purple, the midst thereof being inlaid with love, from the daughters of Jerusalem" (3:9–10).

The description here is not of King Solomon but of the vehicle in which he travels; hence it points to the soul who is a "habitation of God through the Spirit" (Ephesians 2:22, KJV).

The daughters of Jerusalem have seen the glory

of the Lord upon the one now united with Him in His resurrection and seated with Him in the heavenlies. They see that she is entirely His workmanship. Having spoken of His royal litter they now describe this car of state, made by Himself. It is a palanquin for His own personal use, which prefigures the soul whom the Well-Beloved has transformed for His own habitation.

The "wood of Lebanon" speaks of her humanity—"the earthly house of our bodily frame" (2 Corinthians 5:1, mg.); the "pillars of silver" of her redemption at Calvary—redeemed by the precious blood of Christ; the "gold" of the divine life of her indwelling Lord; the "purple seat" of His throne as King. He rejoices in making the place of His feet glorious, so His temple is paved with the love of the daughters of Jerusalem.

The Crowned Christ

> "Go forth, O ye daughters of Zion, and behold King Solomon . . . crowned . . . in the day of his espousals, and in the day of the gladness of his heart" (3:11).

The "daughters of Zion" are bidden to behold the conqueror of Calvary with yet another crown upon His royal brow. The redeemed one is now "a crown of beauty in the hand of the Lord, a royal diadem in the hand of [her] God" (Isaiah 62:3).

These "daughters" may be those of whom it is

written, "Ye are come unto Mount Zion, and unto the city of the Living God" (Hebrews 12:22)—souls who have already been brought into union with the glorified Lord; "overcomers" upon whom He has written the name of the city, the new Jerusalem (Revelation 3:12); members of the Bride, who rejoice to see the Bride-spirit in other souls, and are glad for the gladness of *His* heart.

Chapter 9

"Hath raised us up together, and made us sit together in heavenly places in Christ Jesus" (Ephesians 2:6, KJV).

THE HEAVENLY LIFE

"Behold, thou art fair, My love" (4:1).

The Lord opens His heart to His beloved one who is seated with Him in blessed rest in the heavenlies. He can safely do so now, for she will not appropriate any of His praise to herself.

She has been brought to such deep self-abasement in the wilderness that union with her Beloved in the heavenlies will keep her walking humbly with God—more sensitive to sin, more honest in confession of it, more conscious (in the clearer light of God's holiness) of her need of the blood of sprinkling upon the mercy seat to keep her in unbroken communion with her Lord.

In the time of quiet which followed the conflict and suffering of the wilderness, she has also learned to be silent before the Lord. In the early days, when she was so eagerly longing to know Him, most of the "talking" was on her side; *He* spoke very rarely and briefly. He knew that she would "blaze abroad the matter," and so He could not trust her with more than that which supplied her need.

Indeed, she gave the Lord no time to speak! She entered into His presence, began to talk immediately—poured out her heart—and then left the place of access without waiting to hear His voice or to know His mind.

"My soul, wait thou only upon God, for my expectation is from Him" (Psalm 62:5) is now the attitude of the hidden one. There is silence in her whole being as she abides in her Well-Beloved— the silence of reverence and godly awe.

He speaks from the deep hush of His sanctuary within her soul. Let us listen, as does she, to Him who "quickeneth the dead, and calleth the things that are not as though they were" (Romans 4:17), and let us learn the secret of becoming partakers of the divine nature through the promises (2 Peter 1:4).

The Bridegroom says, "*Thou art fair* "; the soul responds in the humility of faith, "Be it unto me according to Thy word!" (Luke 1:38), and her God becomes her "beauty" (Isaiah 60:19, mg.). She rests upon His "thou art," knowing that He will confirm His word with signs following. She no longer turns toward herself for evidence. She judges Him faithful. His word is sufficient. He is the eternal "I am" who "speaks, and it is done." At the creation of the world He said, "Let there be," and "it was so" (Genesis 1:6–7).

This is the "hearing of faith" that obtains the promises; our "Amen" to His "Yea," for "how many soever be the promises of God, in Him is the Yea: wherefore also through Him [working in us] is the Amen, unto the glory of God through us" (2 Corinthians 1:20).

> "There shall be silence before Thee, and praise, O God, in Zion" (Psalm 65:1, mg.).

"Thou art fair, My love," is the language of the Risen Lord to His redeemed one, as He describes the characteristics of the new life in union with Himself. She is not fair in herself but in Him, for she is a "new creature in Christ Jesus," though as yet far from the full stature of Christ. As she abides in her Lord she will grow continually to a more perfect knowledge of and likeness to her Creator (Colossians 3:10, CH).

The new life must "grow up in every part to the measure of His growth [i.e., to grow into Him is to grow to the standard of His growth] . . . even Christ" (Ephesians 4:15, CH).

The Lord only gives His betrothed the outline which in Him is "Yea"; her part is to "add all diligence" to say "Amen," so that the outline may be filled up with Himself—that at His appearing she may be found "perfect and entire, lacking in nothing" (James 1:4).

The New Creation in Christ

1. Her eyes as doves

> "Thine eyes are as doves behind thy veil" (4:1).

The Holy Spirit appeared at Christ's baptism in the form of a dove. The Beloved beholds the presence of the same Spirit in His betrothed. He sees her as a temple of the Holy Spirit.

She is also a "dove" to the Lord, because she has lost the resentful spirit of the old life; she prays for those who despitefully use her, and in her helplessness makes her nest only in the cleft of the rock (Jeremiah 48:28). Once, in her captivity, she lay among the pots, but now she is to Him as having wings covered with silver and feathers with yellow gold (Psalm 68:13, KJV).

2. Her hair is compared to goats on Mount Gilead

> "Thy hair is as a flock of goats, that appear on Mount Gilead" (4:1, mg.).

The hair of goats in the East is like fine silk. The Nazarite's hair marked him as separated to God (Judges 16:17). Samson's separation to God was the secret of his marvelous strength; when he was shorn of the hair that typified his separation, he was as weak as any other man. So it is in the life of the soul brought into union with the Well-Beloved. Her strength is in the Lord and in the power of His might, and this strength will be manifested only as she abides upon the mount with God, separated unto His will, and for His pleasure.

3. Her teeth are compared to a flock newly shorn

> "Thy teeth are like a flock of ewes . . . newly shorn, . . . come up from the washing, whereof every one hath twins" (4:2).

An old writer suggests that the "teeth" signify the mind or intellectual powers, because the intellect receives and, so to speak, masticates what is given it, as teeth chew the natural food.

The peculiar comparison of the teeth to newly washed and shorn sheep shows us that the Bridegroom means more than a mere description of natural beauty, although primarily the point is the lovely whiteness of the sheep after shearing.

The priests who entered within the veil for ministry were not to enter with woolen garments upon them, for wool suggests the animal or earthly life, and "pure linen" the righteousness of the saints. "The righteousness of God, which is by faith of Jesus Christ, unto all and upon all them that believe" (Romans 3:22, KJV).

The ewes shorn of their wool, which made them delusive in *size* and *weight,* most aptly describes the renewed mind, shorn, as it were, of the wisdom of this world, which fails to "gain by its wisdom the knowledge of God" (1 Corinthians 1:21, CH) and "comes to nought" (lit. "passing away into noth-ingness," 1 Corinthians 2:6, CH note).

Taking the "teeth" to signify the "mind" or the mental powers, may we not gather what is so clearly taught us in the New Testament by St. Paul, that the mind has been "renewed in knowledge"—has come up, so to speak, from the "washing" of the waters of death—in identification with Christ, under the quickening power of the Spirit, to pro-duce double fruit in the new life?*

4. *Her lips are like scarlet, the speech comely*

> " Thy lips are like . . . scarlet, . . . thy speech is comely" (4:3, mg.).

The Well-Beloved "creates the fruit" of her lips (Isaiah 57:19), now cleansed in the scarlet of the precious blood of Christ, purified by the live coal from off the altar of Calvary. Her speech is comely, "such as is good for the building up of the need" (Ephesians 4:29, mg.) of the souls around her, and she knows instinctively that in His presence "fool-ish talking" and "jesting" are not befitting a soul

---

* See Appendix, Note E.

in union with Him. "Be filled with the indwelling of the Spirit *when you speak* one to another" (Ephesians 5:18–19, CH).

5. *Her temples are like a piece of a pomegranate*

"Thy temples are like a piece of a pomegranate behind thy veil" (4:3).

A pomegranate when cut reveals pellucid seeds, like crystal tinged with red, typifying the heart adornment of a meek and quiet spirit, so precious to God, resulting in that stamp of modesty on the brow which calls forth the Bridegroom's praise. The soul is said to be "veiled" because she dwells hidden with her Risen Lord in the heavenly places.

6. *Her neck is like a tower*

"Thy neck is like the tower of David, builded for an armory, whereon there hang a thousand bucklers" (4:4).

Like the woman "made straight" by the Lord Jesus, she was once "bowed together, and could in no wise lift herself up" (Luke 13:11–13). Her glorious Lord has broken the bars of her yoke, and made her to go "upright" (Leviticus 26:13), so that He likens her neck to a tower; yet she is so pliable in His hands that she is the contrary of the one described in Isaiah 48:4: "*obstinate*, thy neck is an iron sinew, and thy brow brass." Neither is she among the daughters who are "*haughty*, and walk with stretched forth necks" (Isaiah 3:16).

The Well-Beloved also compares her neck to the tower of David, which contained the shields of the mighty men of Israel. Her steadfast uprightness, in union with the Lord—"mighty in battle"—makes her invincible, for her shield is God Himself. She is thus prepared for that war with the hosts of darkness which increases in force and intensity as she goes forward in the heavenly life.

7. *Her breasts are like fawns, feeding among lilies*

> "Thy two breasts are like two fawns . . . which feed among the lilies" (4:5).

The fawns are the young of the deer. The breasts, compared to fawns, may signify the *capacity* of the soul for receiving the divine life on behalf of others. This capacity, as yet, is small, and in its present stage capable of little more than receiving nourishment for its own need and the development of its own life. "Everyone that partaketh of milk is without experience of the word of righteousness; for he is a babe" (Hebrews 5:13). "Ye are not straightened in us, but . . . in your own affections. . . . Be *ye* also enlarged" (2 Corinthians 6:12–13), said the apostle.

In the metaphorical language used by the Risen Lord to His purchased one, the characteristics of the new creation as given in the writings of St. Paul are thus clearly traced.

The soul is a temple of the Holy Spirit, recreated in Christ, and built up with all saints "to make a house wherein God may dwell by the presence of His Spirit" (Ephesians 2:22, CH); therefore it is said to have "dove's eyes." It is "strengthened with might by the Spirit in the inner man"; therefore it is able to walk in high places (i.e., heavenly places) as the goats appear on Mount Gilead.

It is "renewed in knowledge," therefore—suggested by the figure of teeth compared to shorn sheep—it has laid aside the wisdom of this world, to be filled with the knowledge of God's will in spiritual—as contrasted with natural—understanding. The lips of the new creation are yielded to God for the utterance of the Spirit. Cleansed in the blood of Christ, they are likened to scarlet, and the speech is comely.

The heart-humility, so beautiful to God and stamping the veiled temples with modesty, is suggested by the cut pomegranate; steadfastness in the faith, by the neck as a tower; and the breasts, likened to fawns, suggest the capacity of the soul for receiving and pouring out of the divine fullness to others.

" If any man is in Christ, there is a new creation: the old things are passed away; behold, they are become new" (2 Corinthians 5:17, mg.).

Chapter 10

"We which live are always delivered unto death . . . that the life also of Jesus may be manifested in our mortal flesh" (2 Corinthians 4:11).

THE RESURRECTION SIDE OF THE CROSS

" Until the day be cool, and the shadows flee away, I will get me to the mountain of myrrh, and to the hill of frankincense" (4:6).*

The soul in union with the Lord, seated with Him in the heavenlies, may be disposed to think now that all "shadows" are over, and that while abiding in the Well-Beloved she will walk in cloudless light.

This is true on the Godward side, for there need be nothing between her soul and God if she "walks in the light as He is in the light," for the blood of Jesus Christ His Son "keeps cleansing" her from all sin.

---

* "Historically, *the hill of frankincense* is Calvary."—Fausset.

But though *inwardly* she moves in the light of the Resurrection Morning, *outwardly* her path is that of the Man of Sorrows when on earth, and must be so increasingly. Outwardly the shadows must deepen in the sorrow that comes through clearer vision of the "mystery of iniquity," and the awful shame of sin against such a God of love. The shadows must deepen until His appearing, when "at evening time there shall be light" (Zechariah 14:7).

In a few brief words the Well-Beloved indicates to the soul that there lies before her a further knowledge of His cross, only possible in the power of His resurrection.

It is significant that such words should follow so quickly after His description of her as a new creation, as if He would remind her:

1. That the *manifestation* of His life will depend upon her continuous resting upon and assimilation to His death; for she must *always* bear about the dying of Jesus, if the life also of Jesus is to be manifested in her mortal body.

2. That in the life of union with the Risen Lord the soul must still go to the "place called Calvary," and must deal with her God upon that ground alone.

3. That, until the day of grace closes with His

appearing, there is a fountain at Calvary open for sin and for uncleanness.

In the "heavenlies" He says to His beloved one, "I will get Me to the hill of frankincense." All through the story *He* is the magnet. He shows Himself at the place to which He desires the soul to be drawn. He will reveal to her His meaning in His own good time. He has yet to teach her what Calvary meant to *Him*, that she may in her measure "fill up the affliction of Christ for His body's sake" and be conformed to the image of the Lamb.

Oh mystery of mysteries, Calvary, dark Calvary! "The sufferings of Christ, and the glories that should follow," are things which the angels "desire to look into" (1 Peter 1:11–12), yet fallen creatures despise and reject the Lamb, the object of all heaven's worship. In eternity alone, purified and freed from the restrictions of the body of clay, shall the redeemed from among men be able to understand the full meaning of His cross of shame and in deepest worship sing:

"Worthy art Thou . . . for Thou wast slain" (Revelation 5:9).

•　　•　　•

The Outlook in the Heavenlies

" Thou art all fair, My love. . . . Come with Me, . . . My bride: look from the top of Amana, from the top of Senir and

Hermon, from the lions' dens" (4:7–8).

For the first time the Well-Beloved calls the soul His *bride*, as if to give her the clearest assurance of her union with Him.

When He desired her to forget everything behind and to follow on to apprehend the "upward calling of God in Christ Jesus" (Philippians 3:14, mg.), He had said, "Come away"; but now that she is united to Him, He is able to say, "Come *with* Me, and look from the top." He would have her look through His eyes from His place of vision and see where He has brought her, that she may triumph in His victory.

From the hour that she said, "I will arise," she has been so occupied with Him that she has altogether forgotten herself, and even her own progress.

After the bitter path through the valley of darkness, when she feared that she had grieved Him beyond repair and that He had forsaken her entirely, she passed by all things and found *Him*. Since then she has given up watching the vineyards and the foxes; she has been quietly intent on doing the will of God from the heart and seeking to walk in the footsteps of her Lord.

Her friends looking on had glorified God in her and had seen that she was being led in the triumph of the King, but she had asserted nothing about herself; she did not know that her face shone, or that the glory of the Lord was seen upon her. She has heard the Well-Beloved speaking to her heart, telling her many things about the new life in union with Him; so when the call comes to "look from the top," she joyfully awakes to the mountain vision.

The Risen Lord bids His hidden one look with Him from the top of Amana (signifying integrity and truth); from Senir (a coat of mail); and from Hermon (destruction). In integrity and truth, covered with the whole armor of God, hidden in Him who was manifested to destroy the works of the devil, she is to look and see that in the triumphant Conqueror of Calvary she is "far above all principality and power" (Ephesians 1:21, KJV), for in His cross He triumphed over "principalities and powers" and put them to open shame.

The "lions' dens" are far beneath His feet; in Him she may tread upon the young lion and the serpent (Psalm 91:13)—for the God of Peace will bruise Satan under her feet as she learns to overcome through the blood of the Lamb (Revelation 12:11).

Chapter 11

"Blessed be the God and Father of our Lord Jesus Christ, who hath blessed us with every spiritual blessing in the heavenly places in Christ" (Ephesians 1:3).

THE BLESSINGS IN THE HEAVENLIES

The glorious Lord now reveals what He is to be in the soul, in the various aspects of the heavenly life, which He describes as manifested in the believer through the power of the Holy Spirit.

The Love of the Spirit

" Thou hast given Me courage, My sister bride; . . . with one look from thine eyes. . . . How fair is thy love, My sister bride! . . . Thy lips, O bride, drop honey; honey and milk are under thy tongue; and the smell of thy garments is like the smell of Lebanon" (4:9–11, mg.).

The heart of Christ is satisfied. Did He not pray to His Father that the love wherewith *He* had loved Him might be in His redeemed ones (John 17:26)?

The *love of God is* now shed abroad in the heart of the hidden one by the Holy Spirit; therefore the Well-Beloved can say, "How fair is thy love, My sister bride."

The believing soul is called His sister because "He that sanctifieth and they that are sanctified are all of one; for which cause He is not ashamed to call them brethren" (Hebrews 2:11), or to speak of "My Father and *your* Father" (John 20:17). She is also a member of His Bride because joined to Him—one spirit.

Moreover, she is now so responsive to Him that one look is her answer to His every call. He tells her that He is encouraged to lead her on, and to "fulfill every desire of goodness, and every work of faith, with power" (2 Thessalonians 1:11). She is becoming fragrant with the sweetness of His presence in her; and the love that fills her heart makes her lips drop words sweet as "honey" and pure as "milk"; yea, her very garments give forth fragrance as the smell of Lebanon.

The Fruit of the Spirit

> "A garden barred is My sister bride; a spring shut up, a fountain sealed. Thy shoots are a paradise with precious fruits; . . . with all trees of frankincense; . . . with all the chief spices" (4:12–14, mg.).

The glorious Lord likens His redeemed one to

a garden enclosed for Himself alone, because she is wholly under His control, to fulfill all the good pleasure of His will.

He has chosen and appointed her to bear fruit (John 15:16), and He sees the fruit of the Spirit, "precious fruits," and all the "chief spices" now appearing (Galatians 5:22). His Father is glorified when there is "much fruit" (John 15:8), for "they shall say, This land that was desolate is become like the garden of Eden" (Ezekiel 36:35); they shall see that the "Hand of the Lord" has done all this— that all is of the Holy One's creating (see Isaiah 41:18–20).

The Living Waters of the Spirit

> "Thou art a fountain of gardens, a well of living waters, and flowing streams" (4:15).

The Beloved makes the believer a "spring shut up," a "fountain sealed," simply that He may be the source of the "flowing streams." He must so guard the soul that it shall never be independent of Him, or able to give forth His life at its own will, or even according to the will of others. It must know that it is helpless apart from Him. He must be the Supreme Possessor, Controller, User, of all that He Himself is within us. Thus would He keep the creature in its right position of dependence upon its Creator.

The Lord now manifests Himself in the redeemed one as a fountain of living water. "The water that I shall give him shall become in him . . . water springing up" (John 4:14), evermore springing up (as unsealed by Him) to become "flowing streams" and "*rivers* of living water" (John 7:38).

What are the conditions of His unsealing?

On the part of the soul in union with the Lord, the continuous abiding in Him indicated by the words: "He that *believeth* into Me . . . out of him shall flow rivers." Not only one single act of faith, but a continual attitude of faith that will keep the soul in Him as its life. He that "believeth *into* Me" (Lit. Gr. John 7:38) moment by moment perpetually, will "abide in Me," and out of him shall flow the rivers of My life.

On the part of others who desire to be blessed, the conditions of the unsealing of the springs are taught us in a picture lesson in the story of the oil that flowed into *empty* vessels (2 Kings 4:2–7), and by the water that filled the "valley full of ditches" (2 Kings 3:16–17, KJV).

When walking in unbroken communion through the power of the blood of sprinkling, and in entire obedience up to light, the believer need carry no care about the "flowing streams," for the Lord knows how to bring needy hearts in contact with the overflow of His life, which breaks forth spontaneously from His hidden ones as they remain restful in His keeping.

The Heavenly Wind of the Spirit

> "Awake, O North Wind; and come, thou South; blow upon
> My garden, that the spices thereof may flow out" (4:16).

The Holy Spirit is likened in the Scripture to "wind" or "breath" (see Ezekiel 37:9, mg.).

The soul is already a temple of the Holy Spirit. It was the Eternal Spirit who imparted to her the gift of life from above, at the very beginning (John 3:8). It was He who cleansed her heart (Acts 15:8–9), took possession of its throne for Christ the King, and caused her to receive Him as a Living Person. It was He who testified to her of the Crucified, Risen and Glorified Lord (John 15:26); and guided her into all truth concerning her death with Him on Calvary's cross and her union with Him in His resurrection and ascension. It was He who brought her out of the sphere of the earth-life into the heavenly realm on the resurrection side of the cross.

Abiding in the clear light of the heavenly sphere, clearly beholding the Risen Lord, the soul is now ready for the breath of God to move upon her, and to use her as never before.

In the sphere of the heavenlies she may now know the working of the Spirit in Pentecostal power, at the will of Him who baptizes in the Holy Spirit and fire. The Holy Spirit is a "rushing, mighty breath" that fills not only the soul but the *house* with His fragrance. It is He who causes the chief spices of the Christ-life to flow out in words of life, "as the Spirit giveth utterance."

The Attitude of the Soul

> "Let my Beloved come into His garden, and eat His precious fruits" (4:16).

This is the first recorded utterance of the redeemed one since she entered into rest with Christ in the heavenlies. She has learned the silence of love, and to be so still that He can speak. In early days she could easily describe her experience; every fresh revelation of Himself was blazed abroad. A few words from Him so overcame her that she could hardly bear them, for she was weak in divine things and needed a wilderness experience to strengthen her before she could know the full communion of the mountain life.

That her Beloved should be satisfied is now her one desire; she can only respond, "Let my Beloved come." The garden is His, the precious fruits are His, all is *of* Him and *for* Him. Her prayer has become the essence of all prayer—a prayer without ceasing!

"Thy will be done."

The Life Abundant

> "I am come into *My* garden, *My* sister, *My* bride: I have gathered *My* myrrh . . . *My* spice . . . *My* honeycomb . . . *My* honey . . . *My* wine with *My* milk."

> "Eat, O friends; . . . drink abundantly" (5:1).

The Spirit-breathed desire of the soul meets immediate response, for the Spirit "maketh intercession . . . according to the will of God" (Romans 8:27).

To the expressed desire of His redeemed one that He will use what He has implanted in her, the Bridegroom gives the quick reply, "I am come." He delicately accepts her reminder that all is His, for He repeats the word "My" again and again—no less than nine times.

He appropriates the precious fruits; and without needing to ask the consent of such a surrendered soul, He turns to the unsatisfied ones around and bids them share with Him the abundant fruit, and to eat of the heavenly food provided by Himself.

> "Eat, O friends, drink abundantly of love."

He will now be able to point to the fainting multitude and to say to the obedient heart, "Give *ye* them to eat."

Chapter 12

"That I may know Him, and the power of His resurrection, and the fellowship of His sufferings, becoming conformed unto His death" (Philippians 3:10).

FELLOWSHIP WITH CHRIST

"I sleep, but my heart waketh: it is the voice of my Beloved that knocketh" (5:2, mg.).

We have in the Song of Songs various photographs, so to speak, of Him in whom dwells all the fullness of the Godhead bodily. The Divine Spirit flashes the light upon Him, first from one point of view and then from another, that the soul may have a complete revelation of Him and be brought into full conformity to His image.

We saw Him first unveiled as "King," taking possession of the throne in the heart, and bringing the will into full surrender and obedience to Him as Lord.

We saw Him next as "The Risen One," approaching the soul from His resurrection glory, inviting her to come out of herself into her hiding place in the cleft of the Rock, her crucified Lord, that she may know that she is joined to Him who was raised from the dead.

We saw Him afterwards as the "Lover" of the soul, rejoicing over the hidden one in her newness of life, and we heard from His lips the characteristics of that life, and of its manifestation to others.

We come now to His revelation of Himself as the "Man of Sorrows," as He invites the bridal soul to prove her heavenly calling by choosing of her own free will to follow Him in His path of rejection, and to be conformed to His likeness as the Lamb.

Though the only begotten Son was appointed "Heir of all things," and was the "effulgence" of the Father's glory, and the "very image of His substance" (Hebrews 1:3), yet, "being found in fashion as a man," He learned obedience by the things which He suffered, and was made "perfect through sufferings" (Hebrews 2:10). The disciple must be perfected as his Master. We are "heirs of God, and joint-heirs with Christ; if so be that we suffer with Him, that we may be also glorified with Him" (Romans 8:17).

The hidden one suggests to us her spiritual experience at this point in the words, "*I sleep*, but my heart waketh." Her whole being is possessed by her Beloved, and dominated by the Holy Spirit, so that she knows now that she is hidden in the cleft of the Rock—the wounded side of the Saviour on Calvary's cross. Consequently the "I" life is so displaced to her consciousness that she can only say in the language of St. Paul, "I have been crucified with Christ . . . it is no longer I that live" (Galatians 2:20, mg.). She is so indwelt and environed by the Lord Himself that she is kept in an indescribable calm. Nothing breaks her rest; she is in perfect peace, stayed upon Him. The fruit of the Spirit—"love, joy, peace, longsuffering, kindness, goodness, faithfulness, meekness, self-control" (Galatians 5:22, mg.)—is so manifested that she is visibly like a "watered garden, and like a spring of water, whose waters fail not" (Isaiah 58:11). The living waters flow spontaneously, and she has heavenly abundance for all the weary hearts who seek her out, drawn to her by the Divine Spirit.

Her cooperation with the Risen Lord is but that of the Vine-Branch: *she* abides in Him, and *He* brings forth the fruit. Often she seems to herself but an onlooker, watching her Beloved doing all through her as she relies upon Him. There is now no struggle or effort. She is, so to speak, "asleep" as to her own *separate* activities, yet never was she more awake to Him, listening for the faintest indication of His will through the Spirit; for the cry of her whole being is: "That I may know Him . . . if by any *means* I may attain unto the resurrection [lit. "out-resurrection"] from the dead. Not that I have already obtained, or am already made perfect," i.e., perfected; "but . . . I press on toward the goal unto the prize of the high calling" (Philippians 3:10–14).

The Voice of the Son of God

"It is the voice of my Beloved that knocketh" (5:2).

The soul failed to understand His voice and movements when He came to her as the Risen One, calling her into fresh knowledge of Himself; but now in the sacred intimacy of unbroken union and communion she has learned to be "of quick scent in the fear of the Lord" (Isaiah 11:3, mg.), for a look or a word between those who are in closest intimacy conveys a meaning no stranger can understand. She knows His voice, and now she intuitively recognizes in its tone a fresh "call," for there is the sound of a "knock" in it.

The Call of the Man of Sorrows

" Open to Me, My sister . . . for My head is filled with dew, My locks with the drops of the night"* (5:2).

---

* "Historically, the agony of Gethsemane. His death is not *expressed*, being unsuitable to the allegory."—Fausset.

Historically, these words refer to the agony of Gethsemane, when "His sweat was as it were great drops of blood falling down to the ground" (Luke 22:44, KJV), and the *spiritual* meaning of the call to the soul, and her response, may be interpreted from that standpoint.

Because she is joined to Him in His resurrection, the Well-Beloved reveals Himself to His betrothed as the Rejected One, that His bride may share His lot and be identified with Him as He *was,* and *is,* in this world. He was rejected when on earth in human form, and He is rejected still. His purchased one must go with Him, and be rejected also, in the world that hates her Lord, if she faithfully cleaves to her heavenly Bridegroom and is truly conformed to His image, following His steps. "I chose you out of the world, therefore the world hateth *you*" (John 15:19).

Based upon this foreshadowing of the Lord as the One who suffered in the agony of Gethsemane, we turn to the picture lesson of this passage in the history of the bridal-soul.

The Well-Beloved stands apparently *without,* and cries, "Open to Me, My sister," as if He said, "You have opened your heart to Me as King, as the Risen One; open to Me now as the One who was 'stricken, smitten of God, and afflicted.' Open to Me that you may enter into the fellowship of

My sufferings, and be made a partaker of My glory."

The Bridegroom cries "Open to Me" because she must always follow Him *by her own voluntary consent and choice*, by the "opening" of her will; but this is the necessary preparation for reigning with Him.

This call is to many wholly unexpected, for they have had such a clear sight of Calvary, and of their identification in death with their Substitute, as to be persuaded that they have entered into its fullest meaning. They expect (and rightly so) an increasing knowledge of the Lord *as the Risen and Glorified One*, on the resurrection side of the cross; but their eyes are not yet opened to see that, in the power of His resurrection, they will know Him in proportion as they enter into the fellowship of His sufferings, "becoming conformed unto His death" (Philippians 3:10).

But the redeemed soul must be truly "in the Spirit," and *established* in its union with the Risen Lord, and fully possessed by the Holy Spirit, ere it is able to rejoice that it is "counted worthy to suffer," and to fill up "that which is lacking of the afflictions of Christ . . . for His Body's sake, which is the Church" (Colossians 1:24).*

---

* "It must not be supposed that the sufferings of Christians now atone for sin. No greater dishonor could be cast upon the work of Christ than that! Nevertheless, Scripture identifies the sufferings

"Many sit at Jesus' table;
   Few will fast with Him,
When the sorrow, cup of anguish
   Trembles to the brim.
Few watch with Him in the garden,
            Who have sung the hymn."

"But the souls who love supremely,
   Let woe come or bliss—
These will count their dearest heart's blood
   Not their own, but His.
Saviour, Thou who thus hast loved me,
            Give me love like this."

---

of Christians with those of Christ. He suffered while hanging on the cross, six hours; He has left one brief hour for the Bride to accomplish, and fill up the perfect number *seven.* He said to the chosen three in the Garden, 'Could ye not watch with Me *one* hour?' (Matthew 26:40)"—Farr.

Chapter 13

"He that loveth his life loseth it; and he that hateth his life in this world shall keep it unto life eternal" (John 12:25).

THE SHRINKING SOUL'S REPLY

"I have put off my coat; how shall I put it on? I have washed my feet; how shall I defile them?" (5:3).

It was such a strange call and revelation of the Lord! The vision breaks upon the soul as to all that it will mean. When He was on earth as the Man of Sorrows, there was no beauty to make others desire Him. "He hid as it were His face" (Isaiah 53:3, mg.)—that is, the out-flashing of His inward glory—so that men hid *their* faces from Him. He was despised; He was esteemed to be smitten by *God* and afflicted.

It has been said that all martyrs have looked mean in their martyrdom. If the cross was stripped of the glory that centuries of worship have thrown around it, we would see more clearly its shame and the depth of Christ's humiliation. It was a blow to the disciples to be identified with their Lord in His hour of shame, and they could not imagine such a development of events even though He had said that He would be delivered into the hands of men. In spite of all His words, it must have come upon them like a thunderbolt, and we cannot gauge the depths of their terror and despair as they all forsook Him and fled.

There is a moment also when, in the illumination of the Spirit, all this breaks upon those who seek to follow the Lord fully, and the meaning of conformity to Christ stands revealed. All preconceived ideas vanish; the soul had thought only of His "power" and "glory," and had overlooked His reminder that the servant is not greater than his Lord, and that the crucified Christ must have crucified followers.

Instinctively the betrothed one shrinks back, not in the purpose of her *will*, but in her humanity.* Maybe she thinks of her Well-Beloved, and of her testimony to others who have glorified God in her. If she follows Him in His path of rejection and sorrow, how can He be shown to others in His

---

* May we not reverently refer in this connection to Gethsemane? Listen to the words of Him who was "God manifest in the flesh," yet perfect man, "in all points tempted like as we are," and hear Him say, "O My Father, if it be possible, let this cup pass away from Me: nevertheless, not as I will, but as Thou wilt" (Matthew 26:39).

glory? She had always thought that He must be made "attractive"! But how can affliction and sorrow be attractive? Moreover, she is indisposed to leave her present experience; she does not know what it may lead to if she accepts His call! Can she not, *may* she not, abide where she is? She is now "sought out," and is being used by Him as a channel of abundant life to others; His glory is so manifestly resting upon her that weary hearts are attracted to Him.

If she follows Him in the pathway of the cross, will these souls still seek her out? What about the offence of the cross? Will the true cross, in its *real meaning* of sacrifice and separation, ever be popular? All these thoughts flash through her mind as she listens to the Well-Beloved's voice.

Note, too, His language to her. He omits the name of "bride" and calls her "sister," "friend," "dove," and "perfect" (v. 2, mg.). His "sister," as doing the will of God; His "friend," because she is in His counsels; His "dove," as hidden in His side; His "perfect" one, because her heart is wholly His. Does the omission signify that her answer will determine whether or not she understands her calling? Whether or not she will apprehend that for which she has been apprehended by Christ Jesus? The Lord knoweth. Let us fear to come short of the fullness of His grace; let us press on toward the prize of His high calling.

In the soul's reply to the Well-Beloved we are also given a hint of the need of a fuller conformity to His death for her own sake! We may discern a little of the "my" creeping in—it may be unawares.

She seems to be appropriating to herself what God has manifested through her, as if it were her own; as if it were something that she had to jealously guard from defilement. She says that she has "put off her coat"—reminding us of the action of Elisha when he took hold of his own clothes and rent them, prior to his taking up the mantle of Elijah (2 Kings 2:12), typifying the rending of the garments of the flesh so that the Spirit of the Lord may Himself clothe the soul.

The betrothed one shrinks back from the call to conformity to the rejected Christ and replies to her Lord that she has *already been to the cross*, "put off her coat," and laid aside the garments of the old life! She knows full well that the foundation of the new life is "I have been crucified with Christ" (Galatians 2:20). But even yet she does not fully understand. He is not calling her now to "put off the old man with his doings" (Colossians 3:9–10), but to enter into the fellowship of His sufferings and be conformed to the image of the Lamb. She has yet to learn in deeper measure that her whole being must be brought into practical conformity to the position already given her in the purpose of God, that she has died in Christ; that "always bearing about in the body the dying [margin, "putting to death"] of Jesus" is the condition of the *"life also of Jesus . . . manifested in* [her] body" (2 Corinthians 4:10).

The soul has already "put off her coat," it is true; but the question "How shall I put it on?" will quickly be answered if she fails to respond to the divine call—for there is no point in the spiritual life where the believer may not drift back, or "build up" that which has been "overthrown" (Galatians 2:18, CH).

However full and blessed the past experience may be, its power depends upon the fresh inflow of the divine life, and the obedience of the soul to the very utmost. The slightest retreat admits the inflow of the old life and is quickly followed by failure and sin.

The fight of faith is to stand firm upon each successive step in the heavenlies, for every step will be contested by the spiritual hosts of wickedness: "having overcome . . . *stand"* (Ephesians 6:13, mg.). Yet the believer dare not stand when God says "Forward," for every call disobeyed means retrogression—and the adversary is ready with the "old coat" under a new name, so that the soul may not know its character.

"I have washed my feet; how shall I defile them?" replies the "friend" to her Lord. The moment she begins to think of protecting herself from defilement, she will need to be shown by the Holy One that He alone is able to keep the feet of His saints. Soul, you are forgetting that in yourself you are black (1:5); in you dwells no good thing; you are but a capacity for God—a "nothing"—that God may be All in all!

The Touch of the Pierced Hand

> " My Beloved put in His hand by the hole of the door, and my heart was moved for Him" (5:4).

The waiting Lord sees the soul shrinking from His call through fear—fear of consequences, fear of losing present blessing—an undefinable fear of what it may all mean in actual suffering. He knows that she is "in great fear, where no fear is" (Psalm 53:5). She should remember all the way He has led her hitherto. His grace has always been sufficient to make each apparently "impossible" step quite easy. She ought to know that the fact of His call proved that He had prepared her for all that He was preparing for her.

He had never bidden her take a step beyond her measure. Why should she hesitate?

If it were a deliberate rejection on the part of her *will*, He could do no more until she yielded;

but He sees that it is only, as it were, a *surface* shrinking, and that she must be enabled to ignore it and to act by her will alone, for in the center of her will she is steadfastly purposed to follow Him at any cost. He therefore puts forth His hand, and immediately her heart is moved.

He knows the character of each of His redeemed ones, and the spring that will respond to the touch of His pierced hand. In some it is the shame of cowardice in leaving to Him alone the path of rejection; in others a high sense of honor in loyalty to their Lord. What spring did He touch in Peter, with that one look that broke his heart?

"My heart was moved *for Him*," says the shrinking soul! Now comes the drawing power of His love. She looks at *Him*, and she forgets her fears. *Him!* That *He* should need her fellowship, and seek it in vain; that *He* should count her worthy to suffer on His behalf (Philippians 1:29), and she shrink back! It cannot be! She is moved for *Him*, and her hesitation is over. She will trust Him! She will follow Him all the way! Her choice is made. "My heart was moved for Him. I rose up to open to my Beloved, and my hands dropped with myrrh . . . with liquid myrrh, upon the handles of the bolt" (v. 5).

"My Beloved is unto me as a bundle of myrrh," the soul had exclaimed in early days at the King's table. As she renews her abandonment and re-opens her whole heart to her Lord, the divine life within her breaks forth in its costly fragrance, as a "sweet savour of Christ unto God" (2 Corinthians 2:15). As the soul chooses the path of sacrifice, her hands—suggesting the hand of faith that draws the bolt of the will—are fragrant with the costly and liquid myrrh.

Chapter 14

"Passing through the valley of Weeping they make it a place of springs; . . . every one . . . appeareth before God in Zion" (Psalm 84:6–7).

THE TRIAL OF FAITH

"I opened to my Beloved; but my Beloved had withdrawn Himself, and was gone" (5:6).

Poor soul! Your hesitation will cost you dear! She opens the door, or abandons herself to Him afresh, but instead of His voice and His face—silence. The Well-Beloved had withdrawn, apparently wounded in the house of His friend.

"I opened . . . but my Beloved had withdrawn Himself, and was gone." The withdrawal of the light of His face now is far more bitter than when He hid Himself before. *Then* it seemed to be without apparent cause, only that she was dull of hearing and had not understood His call. *Now* she is torn with the self-reproach that He has turned away because she did not open to Him immediately.

To a soul in her position of privilege it appears as the blackest crime. She had been brought into such union with Him that He had manifestly sealed her as His own possession. He had given her signal proofs of His love and joy in her; and His glory had been seen upon her by others. That *she* should have hesitated, even in thought, over obeying and following Him at any cost, brings unspeakable sorrow and shame to her heart. No marvel that He has turned away; He is grieved and wounded by the one for whom He has done so much, the one upon whom He should have been able to count to the very end.

How the anguish sweeps over her soul! To her it is sin—blackest *sin*. How could she have dared to speak of having washed her feet, and of fearing to defile herself, when she was grieving Him at the very time? What can she do but fly to the "fountain opened for sin" and humble herself before her God.

The Lord, "excellent in counsel, and wonderful in working," seems to make use of her shrinking (which was not in her *will*), to bring about the fellowship with Him which He desires.

Her detestation of sin, heightened by the knowledge of its exceeding sinfulness as revealed in the light of His holiness, is so deep that she could have borne any suffering so long as she knew that her conscience was void of offence. The agony of having wounded her Well-Beloved is unspeakable. She now confesses that she intuitively knew in the depths of her spirit what His call meant. At the first sound of His voice her soul had failed her, as if it "went forth" from her (v. 6, mg.), and her "spirit fainted" within her (Psalm 142:3, mg.).

The Silent Lord

> " I sought Him, but I could not find Him; I called Him, but
> He gave me no answer" (5:6).

She does not go out into the city to look for Him now; she seeks Him in the solitary place with her broken spirit, desolate and crying in the darkness after Him. It is the darkness over her *spirit* that is now so terrible. In the wilderness path, when she came out of herself to hide in Him, it was simply a darkness that meant no *consciousness* of His presence, no joyous emotion such as she had known in the banqueting house, but she could still rise up with decision, and say, "I will seek Him."

Now her *spirit* is grieved within her. He, who is its very life and light, has hidden His face. Her "spirit is overwhelmed" (Psalm 77:3). She calls to her Well-Beloved, but He is silent. "No answer," to the one to whom He responded so quickly in the past, "Here I am." At last the cry breaks from her in the darkness, "Save me, O God; for the waters are come in unto my soul" (Psalm 69:1).

•　　•　　•

The Well-Beloved is silent. Still His hand will uphold her through all the deep waters; He will bring her out through fire and water into a wealthy place. When the Master heard that Lazarus was sick, He abode still in the same place where He was. He did not move to the help of the stricken sisters until He could say, "Lazarus is dead"; then He said, "I go, that I may awake him." Even so the Lord waits to be gracious to each of His redeemed ones, as He leads them through the deep waters of the way of Calvary.

The Desolate and Tempted Soul

> " The watchmen that go about the city found me, they smote me, they wounded me" (5:7).

She did not ask the watchmen this time if they could tell her about the Well-Beloved. She knew now that she was in the hand of God, and that she must wait His revealings. None could help her, and few would understand her. If she could but have hidden away in her brokenness of heart! But it could not be; she had to move among others as usual, and thus the "watchmen" found her!

They were true, whole-hearted "remembrancers" of the Lord, perhaps (Isaiah 62:6), keenly anxious to be faithful to their calling of warning the wicked to escape from the judgment to come, and of warning the righteous man "that the righteous sin not" (Ezekiel 3:21). When they came upon this desolate child of God, they thought that they saw their opportunity of fulfilling their ministry. "What has happened to this soul that has been so transfigured, so beautiful, so manifestly God-possessed?"

Like Job's friends they gather round, intending to help or comfort, but wounding all the more. "They *talk* to the grief of those whom Thou hast wounded" (Psalm 69:26, KJV), she sobs out to her Lord. "I looked for some to take pity, but there was none; and comforters, but I found none" (Psalm 69:20) is the complaint of her desolation. The darkness over her spirit seems to leave her exposed to wounds from every side. The iron is entering into her soul.

There are other "watchmen" that are also likely to "find" the child of God at such a time as this— the hosts of spiritual wickedness in the heavenly places. It is the hour and power of darkness, the "evil day" of a terrific assault upon the soul. In the hiding of the manifested Presence of Him who not only gives her light but is Himself her Light, the enemy comes upon her like a flood.

They aim at beating her back from her *position* in the Beloved, by attacking her faith in the Faithful God. They press upon her to admit the thought that God has laid upon her more than is right (Job 34:23, KJV) and that she must retreat to an easier path. They taunt her with the silence of her Lord and tell her that if He delighted in her, that if all was right in His sight, He would surely interpose and spare her from all this sorrow.

They present to her some compromise with sin, which would seem to be a "way of escape" from much of the conflict. The attack grows so fierce that it looks as if she *must* yield—it is a "resistance unto blood." Her flesh and her heart fail, but "God is the strength of [her] heart and [her] portion forever" (Psalm 73:26). When the enemy comes in like a flood, the Spirit of the Lord lifts up a standard against him. The soul is strengthened with might by the Spirit in the inner man, to stand steadfast in the faith. She lays the hand of faith afresh upon the head of the Sacrifice on Calvary's cross and waits for God to explain.

The Suffering Soul Laid Bare

"The keepers of the walls took away my veil" (5:7, mg.).

The soul who had walked so alone with her God that others had only seen the outcome of her hidden life had now to face the additional pain caused by the "scourge of the tongue" (Job 5:21). These watchmen, or "keepers of the walls"—active workers in the Lord's service—not only smote and wounded her in their attempts to help her, but took away her veil, exposed her sorrows to others, and laid bare the sacred depths of her soul. Her sensitive spirit knew that they whispered about her, and wholly misjudged the cause of her suffering. They could not know all that had passed in secret between her and the Lord. In her anguish it seemed to her as if her heart had been "unveiled" to the whole world. The "daughters of Jerusalem" (5:8) had also doubtless tried to help her, but how could they understand?

Between the "watchmen," the "keepers of the walls," and these anxious, kind-hearted but meddlesome "daughters," the poor desolate soul felt weary and worn. All the waves and billows break over her; she weeps out in the utter loneliness of her spirit:

" My kinsfolk have failed, my familiar friends have forgotten, . . . my inward friends abhor me: they whom I loved are turned against me. . . . Have pity upon me, O ye my friends; for the hand of God hath touched me" (Job 19:14, 19, 21).*

---

* See Appendix, Note F.

Chapter 15

"He knoweth the way that I take; when He hath tried me, I shall come forth as gold" (Job 23:10).

"Surely I have stilled and quieted my soul . . . my soul is with me like a weaned child" (Psalm 31:2).

THE FAITHFUL SOUL

"I adjure you, O daughters of Jerusalem, if ye find my Beloved, that ye tell Him, that I am sick [with] love" (5:8).

In the depths of her humiliation and brokenness, she who is the purchased one of the Well-Beloved, the joy of His heart, sends a message to Him by the daughters of Jerusalem. She entreats them to speak to Him for her—that is, *if* they find Him, for their access to His Presence is so variable that she cannot be sure when the message will reach Him. Will they tell Him that He is more precious to her than ever, that the "hardness of His love" is as sweet to her as all His favors? Will they tell Him that she is "lovesick" in spite of all the strangeness of His dealings, and of all that He has permitted to come upon her?

When she used this expression before (in 2:5), it was on account of the unspeakable joy of His manifested Presence. That she can use such words *now*, even when He has appeared to withdraw Himself from her, shows us the depth of His work in her and of her union with the Lord. She has stood the test of the fiery trial. She justifies her God and not herself; she kisses the hand that smites her, and glories in the good and acceptable and perfect will of God.

"Blessed is he, whosoever shall not be offended in Me" (Matthew 11:6, KJV). O faithful heart, this blessedness is yours! You have proved that you do love your Lord for Himself alone. You have proved that you do know your God and, "filled with the strength* of faith" (Romans 4:20, CH), can trust Him to do with you as He wills.

You have proved, by His sustaining grace in the depth of your need, that your God is able to make you stand, so that neither the power of darkness nor the misjudgments of the creature can make you doubt your God. You have learned to live in His faithfulness, when "for a little while" you were "put to grief in manifold trials" (1 Peter

---

* Gr. *enedunamothe*—"endynamited."

1:6, mg.). The proof of your faith, proved by fire, is more precious to Him than gold that perisheth, and will be found unto praise and honor at His appearing (1 Peter 1:7).

The Question and Testimony of the "Daughters"

> "What is thy Beloved more than another beloved, O thou fairest among women?" (5:9).

These "daughters," whether they represent professing Christians or true children of God, have evidently never had the Glorious Lord revealed to them or they would not have asked the faithful soul such a question.

To them she is still the "fairest among women," and they do not at all understand the conflict and sorrow through which she has just passed. They have no conception of her anguish over the least unfaithfulness to God and of her fear to grieve Him.

We see, also, that the dread of the bridal soul lest her testimony to the beauty of the Lord should be marred in the path of fellowship with His sufferings was groundless. The "daughters" have seen His glory upon her all the time; His beauty has been revealed through her brokenness. They have seen His humility revealed in her as she reflected Him of whom it was written, "As a sheep that before her shearers is dumb, yea, He opened not His mouth" (Isaiah 53:7). They have marveled at her faithfulness and wondered what her Well-Beloved could be in Himself in order to call forth such devotion as this.

•   •   •

The Soul's Description of the Glorious Lord

> "My Beloved is white and ruddy, the chiefest among ten thousand [lit. "marked out by a banner," i.e., "a standard bearer"] . . . yea, He is altogether lovely" (5:10, 16).

What is her Beloved more than another? The question stirs her whole being. Her Beloved! How can she describe Him who is the effulgence ("emanation," as of light from the sun, CH) of the Father's glory, "the Son of His love . . . who is the image of the invisible God" (Colossians 1:13, 15)?

The bridal soul is moved to the depths of her being. The shadow upon her spirit fades away. The Well-Beloved arises upon her in new glory as the Sun of Righteousness, with healing in His wings (Malachi 4:2). She bursts out with such a vivid word-picture of Him that her hearers, too, are moved.

"My Beloved is white and ruddy," she says, as He breaks afresh upon her soul's vision. He is the Lamb slain in the midst of the throne. "'The Lamb' is at once His nuptial and sacrificial name, characterized by white and red. The Hebrew for *white* is properly *illuminated by the sun*. He is *red* in blood-dyed garment as slain"* (see Matthew 17:2; Isaiah 63:1–2, mg.).

The Apostle John knew the Lord as the Crucified and Risen One many years before he beheld Him in His glory with His face as the sun shining in full strength (Revelation 1:16); and this was followed by a still fuller revelation of Him, through the door which was opened in heaven, as the Lamb in the midst of the throne.

Is this a fresh vision of the Lord that has come to the hidden one because she has followed on to know Him and to be made conformable to His death? It may be so, for she describes Him, for the first time, in the glory of the white light that Ezekiel calls the "terrible crystal" which surrounds the throne of God; yet in the light of heaven he is "ruddy" with the marks of His passion. May we not connect the thought suggested by her words "white and ruddy" and see Him here illuminated to the eyes of her heart as the

LAMB SLAIN—

a "standard bearer" for all who will "follow the Lamb" and be conformed to His likeness?—the Chief among ten thousand, the Firstborn among many brethren.

The faithful soul seems at a loss for language to describe her Well-Beloved, so she gathers to-

---

* Fausset.

gether all that she can conceive of in human beauty to depict her glorious Lord.

He is the one in whom dwells all the fullness of the Godhead bodily; therefore *"His head is as the most fine gold"* (5:11).

She sees Him in His Ascension as in the "dew of His youth" (Psalm 110:3), although He is the "Father of Eternity" (Isaiah 9:6, mg.), the same yesterday, today, and unto the ages; therefore *"His locks are . . . black as a raven"* (5:11).

He is the Lamb "having seven eyes, which are the seven Spirits of God, sent forth into all the earth" (Revelation 5:6); the One in whom is centered the sevenfold vision and power of God the Holy Spirit; therefore *"His eyes are like doves . . . sitting by full streams"* (5:12, mg.).

He is, moreover, the One through whose merits alone can the prayers of all saints be acceptable to the Father, as they ascend like the perfume of the incense compounded of sweet spices— therefore *"His cheeks are as a bed of spices"* (5:13).

His words are spirit and life, every word pure— therefore *"His lips are as lilies, dropping liquid myrrh"* (5:13).

His hand symbolizes His power in action—the "right hand of the Lord doeth valiantly"—therefore to His helpless one *"His hands are as . . . gold"* (5:14), wholly divine in their skillful working.

His body was prepared by His Father to be His tabernacle on earth, and is likened to Solomon's throne made of ivory. "*His body is as bright ivory encrusted with sapphires*" (5:14, mg.).

She sees Him standing up with legs as "*sockets of fine gold*" (5:15) and describes His whole aspect or countenance (KJV) as majestic and glorious. "Yea," she says, "He is altogether lovely" (5:16).

The hidden one is beholding as in a mirror the glory of the Lord, to be transformed into the same image from glory to glory, and she exclaims, "This is my Beloved, and this is my friend, O daughters of Jerusalem!"

The Question of the "Daughters"

> "Whither is thy Beloved gone . . . that we may seek Him with thee?" (6:1).

"It pleased God to reveal His Son in me, that I might preach Him" (Galatians 1:16), said the Apostle Paul. To preach *Him* is very different to preaching *about* Him, even though His Person be the theme. The daughters get a reflected revelation of Him as they listen to the words of the faithful soul and say, "Where is He, that we may seek Him *with thee?*"

"The two disciples heard him [John] speak, and they *followed Jesus*" (John 1:37).

The Soul at Rest in the Beloved

> "My Beloved is gone down to His garden. . . . I am my
> Beloved's, and my Beloved is mine: He feedeth among the
> lilies" (6:2–3).

The first question of the "daughters" drew the soul out of her sorrows to speak of her Well-Beloved. It was then that He immediately arose upon her as the Sun of Righteousness!

Their second question, "Whither is thy Beloved gone?", brings her into her true center of rest, her recollectedness in God, which for the time being she seems to have lost. Why has she been bemoaning His absence and sending Him messages via others, when all the time He has been in His garden? When she shrank from obeying His call, He retreated there, to await the moment when she would respond to Him.

She said He had "turned away," "withdrawn Himself," and was "gone." He had simply veiled His Presence to teach her the cost of withholding anything from such a Lord and that there is no other course but to follow the Lamb when once He has obtained entire control of His purchased one.

She knows now that failing to cooperate with Him in all His will costs far more than any suffering she feared, and that there is no pain so keen as that of wounding His heart.

"My Beloved has gone down into His garden," she replies to the question of the daughters. He is there "feeding among the lilies" of His own life. "I am my Beloved's," the covenant has never been broken, He changes not; with Him "there can be no variation, nor any shadow cast upon me by His turning." He possesses *me*, and He, the glorious Lord, is *mine*.

The soul is now at rest with Christ in God. She does not try to hold Him, as she did when she emerged from the wilderness (3:4); neither does she say, "I have found Him." She simply rests upon the faithful God, who changes not. For a "little while" she thought He was gone, but she has "seen Him again" and knows now that He has been with her all the time. From henceforth she will abide in His love and say, "I am persuaded that neither death nor life . . . nor things present, nor things to come, nor powers, nor height, nor depth, nor any other creation, shall be able to separate us from the love of God, which is in Christ Jesus our Lord" (Romans 8:38–39, mg.).

This is the secret of abiding with Christ in the bosom of the Father. To run after Him presupposes Him as separate from the soul and *as yet to be known* in oneness of life; this would get her out of the right attitude of faith. Should there come a cloud from some failure to respond to His will, or even some conscious transgression, there should not be feverish seeking but a quiet resting on His word and on His changeless love—a sinking down upon His heart in assurance of faith, while trusting Him by the Spirit to apply the power of the blood sprinkled upon the mercy seat and to bring the whole being into stillness again, in the calm of His holy love.

Chapter 16

"For ye died, and your life is hid with Christ in God"
(Colossians 3:3).

THE HIDDEN LIFE

"Thou art beautiful, O My love, as Tirzah, comely as
Jerusalem, terrible as an army with banners" (6:4).

The Well-Beloved speaks again, as the soul rests
in Him, and for the first time He calls her
"beautiful." His eyes already behold in her the
marks of the Bride-city, the new Jerusalem, as she
will come "down out of heaven from God" (Revelation 21:2) in the fullness of time.

The hidden one has passed through deep waters in fellowship with her Lord; and, in the consequent brokenness, her spirit has been freed from
much that kept her from full knowledge of the life
with Christ in God. Now He will teach her how
to dwell with Him in the Father's bosom, and will
open to her the life within the veil.

In the Holiest of All she knows as never before the priceless value of the blood of Christ; she has come not only to Mount Zion and unto the "heavenly Jerusalem," but to "Jesus the Mediator . . . and to the blood of sprinkling" (Hebrews 12:22–24). She sees that the way to God is a blood-sprinkled way, and she knows that through the blood alone can she have liberty and boldness to enter. She is not there by virtue of any past experience of fellowship with the Well-Beloved in His cross; she draws near only through His blood of propitiation, which He carried within the veil, "having obtained eternal redemption for us" (Hebrews 9:12). Through that same priceless blood of the Lamb, sprinkled upon the mercy seat, she will be kept abiding in the Shekinah light—sanctified by the Spirit *"unto obedience* and sprinkling of the blood of Jesus Christ" (1 Peter 1:2).

The soul is now a "hidden one" in the deepest meaning of these words. "Hidden" in the crucified Christ by "faith in the working" of the Holy Spirit, she escapes from the power of the old life and finds that the new has its source in the heart of God. "Hidden" with Christ in God, she must "go no more out" (Revelation 3:12, KJV), until "Christ, who is our Life, shall appear" (Colossians 3:4, KJV), when she, with all who are united to Him, shall be manifested with Him to the world, partakers of His glory.

Following this comparison of His purchased one to the city of the King, we find repeated in the Well-Beloved's language some characteristics of the new creation. These are set forth in verses 5 through 7 and parallel His loving description given previously in chapter 4:1–15, when she was first brought into union with Him as the Risen One and then into the communion of the heavenlies.

Some changes and omissions in using the same figures show us that she is reaching full growth, and is "of ripe age to receive the fullness of Christ" (Ephesians 4:13, CH) and to be taught her heavenly calling more fully by Him so that He may be able to fulfill in her every "good pleasure of His goodness, and the work of faith with power" (2 Thessalonians 1:11, KJV).

1. The worship within the veil

> "Turn away thine eyes from Me, for they have overcome Me" (or "make Me afraid," mg.) (6:5).

The first time the Well-Beloved called His redeemed one "fair" was when He saw the Holy Dove shining through her eyes, the windows of the soul (1:15); and this thought was repeated in 4:1.

Now to His purchased one, brought into assured union with Him, He speaks again of her eyes, but with an entire change of expression. "Turn away thine eyes" is His new request. She is in the place of worship—in the Holiest of All. The seraphim covered their faces as they cried, "Holy, Holy, Holy, is the Lord of hosts" (Isaiah 6:3). A covered face is the appropriate attitude of worship in the presence of a Holy God. Reverence and godly awe must be the marks of the soul admitted to the Holy Place.

"Turn away thine eyes from Me, for they have overcome Me" (lit. "have taken Me by storm"). In her access to the throne of God, she is in the *place of power*, for the eyes of the surrendered one, turned toward Him in helpless weakness and dependence, have power with God.

The Well-Beloved is overcome, conquered, by the speechless cry of one look of appeal from His hidden ones so that He is constrained to answer, "Here I am," and to interpose on their behalf in every conflict. Thus are the hidden ones made "terrible as an army with banners," as they have power and prevail with Him who is a "great God, a mighty, and a terrible" (Deuteronomy 10:17, KJV)—"terrible," as they advance forth from His holy places (Psalm 68:35), to the hosts of darkness.

"Turn away thine eyes from Me, for they make Me afraid" (margin), whispers the Well-Beloved.

"And the Lord said unto Moses, Go . . . charge the people, lest they break through unto the Lord to gaze, and many of them perish." AND A SECOND TIME HE SAID, "*Go*, . . . let not the priests and the people break through . . . unto the Lord, lest He break forth upon them" (Exodus 19:21, 24).

The Lord was afraid *for the people* lest they should not understand His terrible holiness, and should gaze and perish. No man could see His face and *live* (Exodus 33:20).

"Be not highminded, but fear," O child of God, for your God is a consuming fire. Take heed that you cover your face, and walk in godly awe, as you seek to abide in His holy Presence; and remember your ceaseless need of the "blood of sprinkling," which speaks for you upon the mercy seat, as you walk in the light of God.

The Well-Beloved's words, "Turn away thine eyes from Me," may also be taken to signify, in the case of the soul united to Him, a maturity of faith that can walk blindfolded with God (Isaiah 42:19), knowing Him so well that it is content to trust Him without sight, not seeking to pry into His dealings—within in experience, or without in His providence—like a restless child who "wants to know" before it can trust its father. The soul that truly knows God can wait until He pleases to reveal His purposes.

It may also be suggested that the Well-Beloved bids the soul turn away her direct gaze from Him because at this stage she is one with Him and

should take the appropriate *attitude* of "oneness"—
not directing her eyes toward Him, as if she were
separate from Him, but so abiding in Him that
He can enable her to look through His eyes, and
from His standpoint, at what He pleases.

2. *The strength of the hidden one*

> " Thy hair is as a flock of goats, that lie along the side of Gilead"
> (6:5).

The words of chapter 4:1 are exactly repeated,
to signify that the strength of the new creation in
childhood and maturity remains the same. That
is, it has none in itself, but *all in God*. The goats
upon Mount Gilead climb and feed where none
other can find a footing. So this soul finds all
strength in God, and she is able to say, "I can do
all things through Christ which strengtheneth me"
(Philippians 4:13, KJV). Now, as in its childhood,
the secret of the manifestation of that strength lies
in separation to God and in abiding in Him in
helpless weakness.

3. *The renewed mind of the hidden one*

> " Thy teeth are like a flock of ewes . . . come up from the
> washing; . . . none is bereaved among them" (6:6).

The mind or mental powers are again described
under the figure of "teeth," and the glorious Lord
repeats His previous description (see 4:2), omit-

ting only that the "flock" has been "newly shorn."

The understanding has needed *continuous* separation from the intrusion of the wisdom of this world, that it might be taught the wisdom of God; therefore it is said to be "come up from the washing," the "washing of water by the word" (Ephesians 5:26, KJV). Only thus can the mind be continually renewed and be kept so clear and empty that it may be "filled with the knowledge of His will in all spiritual wisdom and understanding, to walk worthily of the Lord . . . bearing fruit . . . and increasing in the knowledge of God" (Colossians 1:9–10).

4. The hidden glory of the soul in union

> "Thy temples are like a . . . pomegranate behind thy veil" (6:7).

Again the Well-Beloved repeats exactly His words of chapter 4:3, showing the life to be a hidden one at every stage. The skin of the pomegranate hides its beautiful interior, which is only seen when cut and laid open. "The King's daughter is all glorious within" by the grace of His presence. But all that she is *in Him*, as she is "accepted in the Beloved," is veiled to a great extent by the earthly house of the body of humiliation. When Christ, who is her life, shall be manifested, then shall she also appear with Him in glory. Then shall He be marveled at in all them that believe.

Meanwhile the high and heavenly calling of the bridal-soul is hidden, yet shown through a simple and lowly exterior. It was written of the only begotten of the Father: "Jesus, knowing that the Father had given all things into His hands, and that He came forth from God, and goeth unto God . . . began to wash the disciples' feet" (John 13:3–5).

When the creature-life seeks to be conformed to the Divine and to be "Christlike," it stoops because it ought, even when contrary to its likings, but does so with an effort; but the spirit of Jesus enables the soul to take the lowest place easily, unconsciously, quietly and habitually, by the power of the indwelling Lord. Moreover, the heavenly life is characterized by increasing simplicity of manner. All outward veneer passes away, because transparency desires no cover. It is genuine, sympathetic, and courteous—not from conventional motives, but because of a true grace that flows from Him who dwells within.

Thus it is with this soul in union with her Lord. The meek and quiet spirit makes her unconscious of herself, as she hides in her Well-Beloved and trusts Him to manifest Himself through her spontaneously and naturally, making her gracefully the servant of all.

Chapter 17

"The mystery of His will . . . to make all things one in Christ . . . in whom we also receive the portion of our lot . . . according to His purpose" (Ephesians 1:9–11, CH).

THE SHULAMITE

" There are . . . queens . . . concubines . . . maidens without number. My dove . . . is but one; she is the only one . . . the choice one" (6:8–9, mg.).

The redeemed one has been brought into union with the King of glory. She worships within the veil. Her strength is in the Lord strong and mighty; He is made unto her wisdom, the wisdom of God. And behind the veil of her lowly exterior, she is beholding as in a mirror the glory of the Lord and is being changed into the same image from glory to glory by the Lord the Spirit.

She has gladly sunk her separate identity in Him, for her sole wish is to have nothing of her own and to be "found in Him" (Philippians 3:9).

She is called the Shulamite (6:13), the "Daughter of Peace"—the feminine of Solomon, the Prince of Peace. She is identified with Him in the eyes of others and shares His name. "This is His name . . . the Lord our Righteousness" (Jeremiah 23:6, mg.); and, "*she* shall be called, the Lord our Righteousness" (Jeremiah 33:16, KJV).

"My dove . . . is the only one, the choice one," says the Well-Beloved to the soul. He speaks of His Bride, the choice one of the Holy Spirit's seeking and preparing. "They two shall be one. . . . This is a great mystery . . . concerning Christ and the Church" (Ephesians 5:31–32, KJV).

He speaks of her as a dove who has hidden in His side—the Cleft Rock of Ages; one who is joined to Him in His risen life, to be increasingly conformed to His image in its purity and meekness.

He says she is but *one*, and His language corresponds to the words in which He expressed to His Father the supreme desire of His heart before He surrendered Himself to the cross—that His prayer might be fulfilled:

> "That they may be one, even as WE are one; I in them, and Thou in me . . . perfected into one" (John 17:22–23).

The heavenly Bride will consist of many souls who have been brought into oneness of life and spirit with the triune God. "Perfected into one," He said, "as Thou, Father, art in Me, and I in Thee, that *they* also may be *one in Us*" (John 17:21, KJV).

Each soul who is one of the many who will form the heavenly Bride will prove her calling and show the Bride-spirit by consenting to "leave all" to follow the Lamb whithersoever He goeth.

This spirit we trace in the Song of Songs, and we also see the faithful heart assured of her union with the Glorious Lord. His Spirit bears witness with her spirit that she has come to Mount Zion, to the heavenly Jerusalem, to the church of the Firstborn, enrolled in heaven.

"One in Us!"

Oh, marvelous words and mystery of God! Can they be written of fallen sinners who have been sunk in the hole of the pit, the horrible pit of sin? The mystery of sin has been met by the mystery of God—God manifest in the flesh, God in Christ reconciling the world unto Himself, followed by "this mystery . . . which is Christ in you, the hope [or assurance] of glory" (Colossians 1:27).

The Well-Beloved describes others in His Father's Kingdom who have not yet entered into the "oneness" of His Bride. There are souls who are "queenly"—noble, victorious ones: these are not like others who are half-hearted, always saying, "Lord, I will follow thee, but . . ." (Luke 9:61, KJV). And yet others, "maidens without number," though *"hidden ones,"* are still babes in Christ, not yet able to bear the fellowship of His cross, or to follow Him in His path of rejection and suffering.

There are also "companions," who follow her when she is presented to the King (Psalm 45:14), on the day when the voice of the multitude in heaven will say, "Hallelujah . . . let us give the glory unto Him: for the marriage of the Lamb is come, and His wife hath made herself ready" (Revelation 19:6–7). And, lastly, there are those who are peculiarly called "Blessed," because they are bidden to the marriage supper.

Meanwhile, the glorified Lord, walking in the midst of His people, rings out the call, by His Spirit, to every blood-bought soul: "He *that overcometh,* I will give to him to sit down with Me in My throne, as I also overcame" (Revelation 3:21).

> *"He that overcometh* . . . I will write upon him the name of . . . *the city* . . . *the new Jerusalem,* which cometh down out of heaven from My God. He that hath an ear, let him hear what the Spirit saith [not to the world but] to the churches" (Revelation 3:12–13).

The Illuminated Vessel of Clay

> " The daughters saw her, and called her blessed; yea, the queens and the concubines, and they praised her. Who is she that looketh forth as the morning, fair as the moon, clear as the sun, terrible as an army with banners?" (6:9–10).

"All that see them shall acknowledge them, that they are the seed which the Lord hath blessed" (Isaiah 61:9). The glorified Lamb has been revealed to the bridal soul. She has seen His glory, as in the mount of God, while hidden in the cleft of the rock (Exodus 33:22). He has made all His goodness to pass before her, and she has come forth with the light of God upon her, so that those around her break out into a description of her as they see her in Christ. Without one word from her, they glorify *Him!* They say, *"Who is she* that looketh forth as the morning?" for they see her in union with Him who is "the hind of the morning," the firstborn from the dead.

Who is she? Just one who would say, "Christ Jesus came into the world to save sinners; of whom I am chief" (1 Timothy 1:15).

Who is she? Just one of those whom God has chosen, those who are described by the Apostle Paul as "foolish," "weak," "base," "despised"— nothings—but in whom Christ Jesus has been made "wisdom from God, and righteousness, and sanctification, and redemption" (1 Corinthians 1:27–30).

The onlookers describe her as "fair as the moon." A most appropriate description, because the moon is a "faithful witness," and this redeemed one is nothing else. The moon is entirely dark in herself and simply reflects faithfully the light of the sun; she remains the same above all the clouds. She moves as her sun moves, wholly dependent upon his upholding power; he is her center and her all. She has nothing apart from him. If he were removed she would sink into space, useless and helpless.

Thus it is with the soul brought into the life of God: she is utterly dark in herself; she has no light but Him. Resting upon the Heavenly Sun as her Center and her All, she moves with Him, and in absolute dependence upon Him, above all and through all the changing scenes of earth. With her soul's vision turned wholly toward Him, her one work is to move in her orbit in the path marked out for her, in correspondence with her Sun.

The onlookers again describe the Shulamite as being "*clear* as the sun," thus emphasizing the words of the Well-Beloved that she is "comely as Jerusalem" (6:4), for the principal characteristic of the Bride-City is its clearness. It is said to be "clear as crystal" (Revelation 21:11), "transparent as glass" (Revelation 21:21, mg.), for it is only a medium for transmitting the glory of Him who is the light thereof (Revelation 21:23).

Moreover, the soul united to the Lord is not conscious of this clear light of God shining through her. If she were to look within to know why the onlookers speak thus of her, she would be dark to herself; she is only "filled with light" as she is occupied with Him who is her Sun.

While "full of light" (Luke 11:34), she is terrible indeed to the works of darkness and to the Prince of darkness; she is terrible as an army with banners, for clothed in the armor of light she is one of the souls of whom it is written, "they overcame him by the blood of the Lamb, and . . . they loved not their lives unto the death" (Revelation 12:11, KJV).

She becomes more and more an illuminated vessel of clay through which her Lord will show Himself again to weary hearts lying in darkness and the shadow of death. She is increasingly being prepared for the hour when her body of humiliation will be conformed to the body of His glory, according to the working whereby He is able to subject all things unto Himself.

Chapter 18

"Who is blind as he that is at peace with Me, and blind as the Lord's servant!" (Isaiah 42:19).

THE SOUL'S FAILURE IN ABIDING

" I went down into the garden . . . to see the green plants . . . to see whether the vine budded. . . . Before I was even aware, my soul set me among the chariots of my princely people" (6:11–12, mg.).

The Shulamite has now to learn the conditions of abiding in the light of her Lord's countenance. She is not yet established in this degree of union, nor does she know all its special dangers, or the wiles of the adversary at this stage of the spiritual life.

The hidden one quickly learns how *not* to abide, for she says, "I went down into the garden to *see!*" This, in practical experience, means self-introspection, which immediately brings a cloud upon the soul. *She* is the Lord's garden; it is not her place to go down to see how the Lord's plants are growing. In other words, she must not look at her own experience or be occupied with how she is "getting on," but she must be obediently "looking unto Jesus" (Hebrews 12:2). This is her part alone.

It is not without reason that the Lord always mentions *first* the "eyes of the heart," for they indicate the main attitude of the soul, and upon *their* faithfulness depends the "abiding." If "thine eye be single, thy whole body shall be full of light" (Matthew 6:22). The Shulamite must learn that the single eye is blind to all else but the will of God; she must be content not to "see" other things if she is to abide in her Lord.

We may also think of the "garden" as Christian work with which the hidden one is deeply concerned. She wanted to see whether there were signs of fruit, and so she "went down into the garden." She has yet to be taught that she may not act independently of her Well-Beloved in the smallest matters; for little things are very great in their consequences. The right thing may be done at the wrong time. He would have her concerned in His gardens, and in the budding vines, but she must not go until she is sent; she must learn to walk in step with Him, and to know that those who truly believe in His all-wise working are content not to "make haste" (Isaiah 28:16) but to await His will.

The Shulamite tells us frankly what she did, and how quickly she found out her mistake. Possibly the chorus of the onlookers distracted her a little from the still small voice of her Lord. Whatever the cause, in the assurance of her union with Him, probably without "inquiring at His mouth," she went down to have a look at how things were going on in the "work"! Maybe it was because of her natural activity and energy that she was one of those souls so difficult to bring into the stillness and rest of God.

"Just a peep," she said to herself, and before she knew it she found herself swept into a whirl that she likens to "chariots"; she had missed the Lord's path and had lost her deep, centered calm.

But who are the "princely people" who were the immediate cause of this? Possibly souls knit to her in a special spiritual tie, her own children, who have become princely souls (Psalm 45:16); or others who had been changed from "Jacobs" to "Israels," spiritual princes having power.

Oh soul, you will have to learn to be both blind and deaf if you are to walk continuously in the will of your God and thus to abide in the Holiest of All.

The Call to the Shulamite

"Return, return, O Shulamite; return, return, that we may look upon thee" (6:13).

The soul united to the Lord is made quickly conscious of a step out of His will, and is so readily obedient that to see her mistake is to retrace that step without hesitation; and to retrace means an immediate confession of sin, and restoration through the precious blood of Christ.

The language of this call shows us that the Shulamite has fled to her hiding place in the sanctuary of God. She could not delay a moment— she must get back into step with her Beloved, whatever it means.

She is hidden secretly in His pavilion from the clamor of tongues that follow her, "Return, return, that we may look upon thee." They who call are loath to lose her and are in danger of clinging to the vessel illuminated by the Lord—for indwelt by Him, she is pressed upon by the multitude with their needs. She is "sought out, a city not forsaken" (Isaiah 62:12). The Beloved has fulfilled His promise: "Thy life shall be clearer than the noonday . . . yea, many shall make suit unto thee" (Job 11:17–19).

The Bridegroom's Question

"Why will ye look upon the Shulamite, as upon the dance of Mahanaim [or "two companies," mg.]?" (6:13).

The Well-Beloved replies* to these souls on behalf of His hidden one, because "all things are naked and laid open before the eyes of Him with whom we have to do" (Hebrews 4:13). He asks a question! *"Why* will ye look upon the Shulamite?"

What are your *motives,* eager souls? Do you want the Shulamite, or the Shulamite's Lord? He gently rebukes that element of the earth-life which His eyes of fire behold, as He adds, "Why will ye look upon the Shulamite, *as upon the dance of Mahanaim?"* His word is quick and powerful, and pierces "to the dividing of soul and spirit" and is "quick to discern the thoughts and intents of the heart" (Hebrews 4:12). Their desire to look upon this God-possessed one is not wholly pure; she is attractive to them in some measure because she pleases their eyes and gives them pleasure.

The word "Mahanaim" means "two hosts," and it was a name given by Jacob to the place where the angels of God met him (Genesis 32:1–2). "Why will ye look upon the Shulamite, as *upon two hosts of angels?"* Does the Well-Beloved see the eager hearts thinking of her "above that which is written"? St. Paul said he would not speak of the

---

* This may be also the reply of the soul to the call, "Return." In either case she is one with her Lord; she has fled to her hiding place in Him, and if she speaks, it is because she has been "sent" by her Beloved with the question that lays bare the hearts of the eager ones who desired her to "return."

glory of the revelations of Christ to him, "lest any man should account of me above that which he seeth me to be" (2 Corinthians 12:6), a sinner saved by grace!

Chapter 19

"We are His workmanship, created in Christ Jesus for good works, which God afore prepared that we should walk in them" (Ephesians 2:10).

THE SOUL EQUIPPED
FOR SERVICE

"How beautiful are thy steps . . . O Prince's daughter! [Thou art] the work . . . of a skillful Workman" (7:1, mg.).

In reply to the question "Why will ye look upon the Shulamite?" the eager onlookers who beg her to return describe the redeemed one as they behold her equipped for service.

They see her as the work of the hands of a skillful Workman, and call her blessed; they show that they are beginning to understand her separation unto the Lord and her inability to please men, and that she is the faithful servant of Christ. She cannot "return" unless she is "sent"!

The Well-Beloved has used His hidden one before. We have seen His joy over the "precious fruits" and "rivers of living water"—the spontaneous outflow of the abundant life. At that time the soul did not understand the conditions of His working through her and how she was intelligently to cooperate with Him as a fellow-worker. She is now of full age to receive the fullness of Christ, and she must know the solemnity of being called to work with God, that His fullest purposes through her may not be hindered by her ignorance.

In the language by which the "princely people" (or the "daughters") describe the Shulamite, we may trace the characteristics of the prepared fellow-worker and the conditions of effective service in cooperation with God.

1. Step by step in the Spirit

"How beautiful are thy steps" (7:1, mg.).

The Shulamite has returned to her abiding place and is now seeking to walk "step by step in the Spirit" (Galatians 5:25, Moule). She is the workmanship of a "skillful Workman" who has created her anew in Christ Jesus. She will not need to run hither and thither now and plan for herself, because He has prepared a path of service for her. The "skillful Workman," who is almighty, has prepared the worker and the work. The plan will be kept in the hands of the Master Workman, and by the skillfulness of His hands upon her He will guide her moment by moment in the prepared path and increasingly prepare her for each new step as she walks with Him.

Her feet will be beautiful if she thus walks with God, and she will find that the sandals He has given her—"the preparation of the gospel of peace" (Ephesians 6:15), peace within and peace around, keeping her stayed upon Him in perfect peace—protect her from contact with the earth. All grace abounds for her—all she needs, if she agrees to walk in the way of His steps: not going down to see the vineyards until she is bidden, but content to do the next thing like a little child.

2. Strengthened with heavenly food

> " No mingled wine wanting . . . wheat set about with lilies" (7:2).

The "wine of the New Testament is His blood."* The "wine" and the "wheat" referred to here remind us of the words of the Lord:

> " My flesh is true meat, and My blood is true drink. He that eateth My flesh and drinketh My blood abideth in Me, and I in him. . . . He that eateth Me . . . shall live because of Me" (John 6:55–57, mg.).

The quickening life of Him who is a "life-giving Spirit"—signified by the wine—must never be

---

* Fausset.

lacking if the soul is to be strong in the Lord and in the power of His might.

His flesh is the "bread of life" and is the heavenly substance provided as "food for the new man"—suggested by the "heap of wheat." If she would not be "weak and sickly," but in her weakness be made strong and "wax mighty in war" (Hebrews 11:34), she must be taught by the Spirit to "discriminate . . . the body" (1 Corinthians 11:29–30, mg.) and to feed upon Him in her heart "by faith with thanksgiving."

Feeding upon and assimilating the "true meat" and "true drink" day by day, she will find her food supplied to her in doing the will of God, even as the weary Son of God in the days of His flesh was fed with heavenly food while meeting the need of one sinful heart. "The disciples prayed Him, saying, Rabbi, eat. But He said . . . I have meat to eat that ye know not. . . . My meat is to do the will of Him that sent Me" (John 4:31–34).

3. Her capacity for God

"Thy two breasts are like two fawns" (7:3).

The capacity of the soul is again spoken of under the figure of the "breasts," and it is significant that the fawns are not said to be now "feeding among the lilies" (4:5). "There are two kinds of capacity. (1) A capacity proper to the creature, which is small and limited. (2) A capacity of being lost continually more and more in God.

"The melting process through which [the soul] has passed has taken from him all form (which compressed him within the rigid limit of his own capacity) and disposes him to flow into God, as water joined to its sources blends with it ever deeper and deeper. (This does not mean that he loses his nature as a creature, and that God could not cast him forth again—although this is what He will not do.)"*

The purchased one has been brought, in union with her Beloved, to be "hid with Christ in God." As she abides in Him as her dwelling place, she will be able to give out of His fullness to needy souls, for she is no longer straitened in herself, or in her own affections. "Open your hearts to us," or "Make room for us" (margin), said Paul to the Corinthians (2 Corinthians 7:2). There is room in her heart for all for whom Christ died, and as her capacity is continually increased by His hand upon her, His fullness will flow into her, and through her, as she pours out to others.

4. Unswerving obedience to God

"Thy neck is like the tower of ivory" (7:4).

Her neck is described as a "tower of ivory,"

---

* *Life Out of Death* (CLC Publications).

suggestive of steadfastness. Once it was as iron, because she was so obstinate (Isaiah 48:4). Now it is compared to ivory, because it is changed to unswerving, faithful obedience to the revealed will of God. As a "fellow-worker with God" she is set by Him as "a tower and a fortress" among His people (Jeremiah 6:27), "that thou mayest know and try their way." She must be meek and yielding in all matters concerning herself, but be as a "tower of ivory," unbending, in faithfulness to her Lord.

5. *Stillness of heart to hear the voice of God*

"Thine eyes as the pools in Heshbon" (7:4).

From the beginning of her history, the different expressions by the Well-Beloved concerning the "eyes of her heart" have been the gauge of her growth in the divine life. The eyes are now compared to pools in their clear, still depths, showing how the inner life has been brought into the deep calm of God. She has learned to be still and know her God.

No need of "earthquakes" now to tell her that the Master Workman is working salvation in the midst of the earth; she is able to hear the "sound of gentle stillness" (1 Kings 19:12, mg.) in her heart as He makes her to know His will, so that she may be His instrument to teach His people "the difference between the holy and the common, and cause them to discern between the unclean and the clean" (Ezekiel 44:23).

While she abides in her Beloved she is given discernment of spirit in the stillness of her heart, so that she may not judge after the flesh and the sight of the eyes but in the sanctuary and light of God.

6. Intuitive scent in the will of God

"Thy nose is like the tower of Lebanon" (7:4).

The "nose" has not been spoken of before, because the "scent" is one of the senses of the new creation which only seems to be recognizable in the stage of maturity, and seems the quickest to be dulled by any act out of His will. The God-man was said to be "quick of scent in the fear of the Lord" (Isaiah 11:3, mg.). The "scent" implies that exceedingly delicate intuitive knowledge of God which can only be likened to the sense of smell. The nose is said to be like a "tower," because this quick scent can only be maintained as the soul walks in His will in steadfast obedience and abides in the rarefied atmosphere of the most intimate fellowship with Him.

7. Power with God to prevail with man

"Thine head . . . is like Carmel, and the hair . . . like purple; the King is held captive in the tresses thereof" (7:5).

Her head is compared to Carmel, the mountain where Elijah had power with God and prevailed with man. "The hair . . . is like the purple of a king, bound in the tresses thereof" (margin).

How beautifully this suggests the "royal priesthood" of those who are loosed from their sins in His blood and made "kings and priests" unto God (Revelation 1:5–6, KJV)—separated to minister within the veil with their Great High Priest on behalf of the people.

The hair—the figure of strength (as illustrated in the case of Samson)—is now described as having royal power, holding captive the King himself. Thus did clinging Jacob hold the God-man on the lonely hillside. "By his strength he had power with God: yea, he had power over the angel, and prevailed: he wept, and made supplication unto Him" (Hosea 12:3–4, KJV). His strength lay in his weakness; he could only cling, and dare to hold captive the King of kings in human guise. He dared to say, "I will not let Thee go, except . . . !" and thus he had power with God and could prevail with man.

The soul in union with the Well-Beloved will now be taught how to move men *through God*, rather than, as heretofore, by seeking grace *from* God to move them *for* God! She will "stand before God for the people" (Exodus 18:19, mg.) by dwelling

under the Shekinah light; "accepted in the Beloved," she will "move the hand that moves the
world" by holding the King captive with His own
written word and humbly crying, "Do as Thou
hast said."

The Work of a "Skillful Workman"

> "How fair . . . art thou. . . . This thy stature is like to a palm
> tree, and thy breasts to clusters of grapes" (7:6–7).

"How fair and how pleasant art thou," exclaim
the onlookers as they gaze upon the workmanship of the Divine Workman. He has brought her
to know a moment-by-moment dependence upon
Him that will keep her in His will; her capacity
for Him is being enlarged day by day, so that the
fruit which He brings forth is as clusters of grapes.
She is now at His disposal in truest selflessness;
she is a tower for Him in immovable steadfastness. He has brought her whole being into the stillness that is essential for His fullest working. He
has taught her the quick perception of His will.
He has given her to know that strength of faith in
His word which will hold the King captive to per-
form it.

"Thy stature is like to a palm tree" is the ver-
dict of those who call her blessed, for she has
reached the measure of "manhood" and is as a
pillar in the house of her God.

"The palm tree is an upright, fruit-bearing tree. It will not be pressed or bound downward, or grow crooked, though heavy weights be laid on it. The more it is oppressed the more it flourishes; the higher it grows, the stronger and broader it is in the top."*

"The righteous shall flourish like the palm tree" (Psalm 92:12), said the psalmist of those who are "planted in the house of the Lord." The growth is rapid in the clear atmosphere of the mount of God and in the sunshine of His face. The life of God cannot be bound, or turned aside into crooked ways. It can have no fellowship with darkness. By its very nature, however much it may be oppressed and despitefully used, it will spring higher and stronger into the pure air above the things of earth and bear fruit unto God.

A Listening Soul's Desire

" I said, I will climb up into the palm tree, I will take hold of the branches thereof" (7:8).

There were probably others listening to the description of the "Prince's daughter" as one in union with the Lord and a fellow-worker with Him.

One listening soul, moved with desire for the same fellowship with the Well-Beloved, breaks out with the words, "I will climb up!" No, eager heart, that is not the way; you must first "climb" *down*.

* Cruden.

You say, "I will take hold of the branches." No! Of what use can that be? Why take hold of the *branch* when you may have the *sap*—the divine life that flows freely through the Lord's palm tree?

Many have "taken hold" of the Lord's palm trees, and hang upon them. But put to the test, they show that they know little about the solitary walk with the Well-Beloved through the valley of the shadow of death, into the calm of the life with Christ in God.

Alas for the "climbers" in the day when God will shake all things, that those "things which cannot be shaken may remain" (Hebrews 12:27, KJV).

Oh seeking soul, it is well that you desire a like fellowship and conformity to the image of the Well-Beloved, such as you see in His possessed ones; but you must go "solitary" (Numbers 23:3, mg.), and yield wholly to Him with fixity of heart to follow Him wherever He goes—and then you shall know the Lord.

"Be it so," replies the eager heart, as she turns to the Shulamite and speaks to her thus:

> " Let thy breasts be as clusters of the vine . . . the smell of thy nose like apples . . . thy palate like the best wine, that goeth down aright . . . causing the lips of those that are asleep to speak" (7:8–9, mg.).

It's as if she were saying, "Let your capacity be ever more increased as you pour out draughts of the fullness of your Well-Beloved to needy hearts, and let Him find abundance of fruit upon you, even as the clusters of the vine.

"Let your 'scent' in the fear of the Lord grow stronger and stronger, even as the smell of apples— as the scent of your Well-Beloved, whom you likened to an apple tree among the trees of the wood.

"Let your 'taste' for the new wine of the Kingdom, the best wine kept even until now, be ever sensitive and true. Thus shall your lips be caused to speak as you are in the deep rest of God, asleep, as it were, to all but Him, who is your strength, your All."

Chapter 20

"God's fellow-workers" (1 Corinthians 3:9).

"Workers together with Him" (2 Corinthians 6:1, KJV).

"The Lord working with them" (Mark 16:20).

GOD'S FELLOW-WORKER

"I am my Beloved's, and His desire is toward me. Come, my Beloved, let us go forth into the field" (7:10–11).

Following the description of the believer as "His workmanship, created in Christ Jesus for good works," these words spoken by His hidden one are most appropriate. Her attitude is one of restful faith; she says, *"I am my Beloved's,* I am at His entire disposal, separated unto Him and unto the gospel (Romans 1:1). In the shadow of His hand He has hidden me; He has made me a polished shaft (Isaiah 49:2). *His desire is toward me;* His will is to use the vessel He has thus prepared. And His desire toward me moves in me *toward Him. Come, my Beloved;* I may not, I dare not, go without Thee. Come, *let us go forth* into the field, the great field of the world!"

The soul hidden in His hand says nothing now about herself; she is wholly taken up with Him and His desire. This is the divine remedy for self-consciousness and shyness. A God-consciousness that excludes the remembrance of self bestows the highest culture and the truest grace. The inward revelation of Christ had this effect so long as His presence was powerfully *manifested* to the consciousness; but abiding deliverance comes from such a knowledge of one life in common with the Well-Beloved that the soul is drawn out of itself, so to speak, to dwell in Him.

We see this exemplified in the experience of the Shulamite. In early days, even though Christ was "dwelling in her heart by faith," she was still disposed to the "self" center which grasps to itself all things and sees them only in their relation to itself. She manifested this in her words, "My Beloved is mine!" "I am *His*" was a secondary thought (2:26).

Later on, we watch her losing her "self" center as she rests upon His hold of her and says, "I am my Beloved's, and my Beloved is mine" (6:3).

Now even the "mine" has vanished, for she is centered wholly upon Him. He fills her whole mental and spiritual vision. What *she* has, what *she* is, what concerns *herself*, is all out of the range of her consciousness. That *He* may have His way; that *His* heart's desire may be fulfilled; that *His* inheritance in the saints may be given Him; that she may be all *He* wants her to be—this fills her mind and thoughts. He will care for her and will fulfill her every need; and she only needs what *He* thinks she needs. She only desires what He desires, and what He will desire in her.

Oh happy, happy soul! Your sun shall no more go down, for your God is your glory and your exceeding joy. "As the bridegroom rejoiceth over the bride, so shall thy God rejoice over thee" (Isaiah 62:5).

She is now God's fellow-worker in service.

Her Enlarged Vision

"Come, my Beloved, let us go forth into the field" (7:11).

The world lies before her in the light of God. No longer can one little corner of the vineyard be more important than the rest. "*My* church, *my* mission, *my* cause" has given place to the great field of the world. She has heard her Well-Beloved say, "Other sheep I have, which are not of this fold; them also I *must* bring, and they shall hear My voice" (John 10:16), and she has entered into fellowship with His great heart of love. She knows

His "must" in this is as imperative as the "must" that led Him to Calvary (John 3:14; Matthew 16:21).

She knows, too, that His Father said to Him, on the day that He sat down on His right hand as the conqueror from Calvary, "Ask of Me, and I will give Thee the nations for Thine inheritance, and the uttermost parts of the earth for Thy possession" (Psalm 2:8).

Intense yearnings possess her soul; she begins to "strive" in prayer for those whose faces she has never seen, longing that their "hearts may be comforted" as hers has been, and that they may "know the mystery of God, even Christ" (Colossians 2:1–2).

Her Pilgrim Spirit

"Let us lodge in the villages" (7:11).

She is now so free in spirit and heart that she can move about quickly just as He pleases. A "lodging" will do, for her home is in Him. She has many times said, "Whither Thou goest, I will go; and where Thou lodgest, I will lodge" (Ruth 1:16). Now He must lead her forth and fulfill His promise: "Every place whereon the sole of your foot shall tread shall be yours" (Deuteronomy 11:24). The lands must be claimed for Him; for they will yet become the kingdoms of our Lord and of His

Christ. Like Abraham, she is content to be a pil-
grim and a stranger, to sojourn in tents in the "land
of promise" which she will afterward receive as
an inheritance when she will reign with Him. "The
meek shall inherit the land; and shall delight themselves in the abundance of peace" (Psalm 37:11).

Her Diligent Activity

> "Let us get up early to the vineyards" (7:12).

There is no room for sloth in a life of obedience. There is ceaseless activity in the realm of
the King of kings. "My Father worketh hitherto,
and I work," said the Lord Jesus when He was on
earth in human form. If the angels are given charge
over His hidden ones, to "keep them in all their
ways" (Psalm 91:11), they have much to do. There
is a "creaturely activity" that hinders God, and a
"passivity" that is *not* of God, a passivity that is
only another name for sloth. When the Lord is
permitted to still the "fuss" and activity of the creature, and to bring the soul into restful cooperation
with Him, He is able then to work through His
instrument "*mightily*" (Galatians 2:8, KJV)—the soul
adding, on her part, all diligence. This includes
even "getting up early," as the Master did, to see
to the vineyards—but first of all, by intercession
within the veil!

Her Joy Over Souls

> "Let us see whether the vine hath budded, and the tender grape appeareth, and the pomegranates be in flower" (7:12, mg.).

Once she went to see if the vine was budding without asking at the mouth of the Lord, and found herself out of her hiding place. Now she says, "Let *us* see!" She has always had a keen passion for souls, but formerly her "own" activity used to draw her out of step with her Lord. Now she fears to move without Him, and if she will always ask His will, He will keep her in the way of His steps. She may "look on the fields . . . white already unto the harvest" (John 4:35) when she looks with Him; and in union with Him, she will see the grace of God and be glad. She will be able to discern the first tokens of fruit, and the blood-red flower of the pomegranate will be a special joy when seen in His own children—for it indicates the hidden beauty of the bridal souls who satisfy His heart.

Her Fellowship With Her Lord

> "There will I give Thee my love" (7:12).

It is blessed to see how this hidden one is growing in the knowledge of her Lord. There was so much of "me" and "my" in those early days (2:3–6).

Then it was, "My Beloved is unto *me*" (1:14).

Now she says, "There will *I give Thee my love*"; in effect, "Give the love Thou hast implanted in me back to Thee, by pouring it out on those for whom Thou hast died." "Unto the least of these My brethren . . . *unto Me*" (Matthew 25:40), the Master said. In binding up the broken-hearted with His word of healing, in proclaiming His liberty to the captives, in comforting all that mourn with the comfort of God, her life *is love;* and love—*His* love—is satisfied!

She has also learned to be "at home" in the sanctuary of His Presence everywhere. "*There,*" in the midst of ceaseless service, He is with her, and "there," in pouring out to thirsty hearts she gives Him to drink.

Her Open Doors

"At our doors are all manner of precious fruits . . . which I have laid up for *Thee*, O my Beloved" (7:13).

"For *Thee*," again comes from her lips, "precious fruits . . . for *Thee*." She has eyes to see all manner of precious fruits in others now. Once she could only recognize one special kind of fruit as acceptable to Him, and expected to see it on every one of the Lord's "trees"! Now she knows better the individuality of souls, and can discern "all manner" of fruit produced by the new life in union with Him, for "the fruits of light are in all goodness, and righteousness, and truth" (Ephesians 5:9, CH).

She discovers, also, that as she walks in the prepared path of service she does not have to run hither and thither for opportunities of gathering His precious fruits. Day by day, all is at her door. She will need the most vigilant faithfulness to gather what is brought to her hands, to redeem the time, and to buy up her opportunities.*

---

* Literally, to buy up an article out of the market, in order to make the largest possible profit from it (CH).

Chapter 21

*"How much more shall the blood of Christ . . . cleanse your
conscience . . . to serve the living God?"* (Hebrews 9:14).

THE SOUL "OUT OF TOUCH"

"Oh that Thou wert as my brother. . . . When I should
find Thee without . . . I would lead Thee" (8:1–2).

Beloved of the Lord, what has happened to
you?

These words are such a contrast to her last ones!
Some change has evidently taken place. We saw
her in the joy of blessed service with the Well-Beloved; His desire was toward her, and her fellowship was so intimate with Him that she could freely
say, "Let *us* go forth!" Now she speaks of Him as
though He were *"without,"* and as if she had to
lead Him to her home!

She must be out of step again. Possibly some
subtle thought of self-confidence has caused her
to miss the path, and she was unaware of its first

approach. She did not know the danger of it. The Well-Beloved is teaching her how to abide in Him, and she must learn that notwithstanding all the way in which He has led her, she is not in a state of permanent blessing. His workmanship brought her simply to a place of utter dependence, and to an *attitude toward Him* in which He could be All in all.

She has learned the lesson that she must not act apart from Him. She probably missed step with Him, by thinking that she knew how to abide!

It is difficult to be emptied of our own wisdom; it is more difficult to be *kept* emptied! It is not easy to be so thoroughly detached from all previous knowledge as to hang in helpless dependence upon our God, and to expect Him to be continually made unto us Wisdom. The very knowledge given by God in the first instance, if grasped and clung to as our own, may keep us from understanding His fuller revelations later on in the spiritual life.

At every stage it is only possible to say, "I know in part, but *then* shall I know fully, even as also I have been known" (1 Corinthians 13:12, mg.).

The Danger of Self-Effort

"Oh, that Thou wert as my brother . . . I should . . . I would . . . yea, I would!" (8:1–2).

The first intimation that the soul is out of touch

comes from the silence of the Lord—silence in the heart and in the written Word, for the written Word is the expression of the Living Word and is His language of communication.

We have seen in the history of the hidden one that the Lord is sometimes silent to test our faith, so that we may learn to trust Him apart from His voice, or His manifested Presence. But the soul has then a deep inward rest and conviction that it is in the hand of God; it knows that He is not habitually silent, and will bring all who rely upon Him as they "walk in darkness, and have no light" (Isaiah 50:10) into fuller communion with Him as they follow on in the path of His will.

The Shulamite is not at rest; she intuitively knows that His silence indicates that she is out of step, and this is a call to her to wait at His feet so that she may be shown the cause.*

Her words show us that she is in danger of getting into agony and "struggle" over her loss of "touch," and indicate that the sense of homelessness from being out of her hiding place is unbearable. For the moment she wishes she could only *see* her Beloved as a human being—a tangible person, like her brother—so that she could take hold of Him, and lead Him to a quiet place to obtain His instruction.

---

* See Appendix, Note G.

But all in vain, poor soul! It cannot be in your way—no self-effort will do. To struggle will but increase the sense of separation, and bring worse matters in its train. Be still, and by faith shelter afresh under the blood of sprinkling. Thus He will teach you His way.

The soul gives a hint that she has been despised (8:1); possibly she had said too much about her fellowship with the Well-Beloved and she had been considered "presumptuous" or even extravagant in her devotion and obedience to Him. She has forgotten that although her inward life has been illuminated by the Sun of His glorious presence, she has never been promised anything but suffering, tribulation, and rejection in the world that rejected Him. The God-man made no secret of this to His disciples, but said, "Blessed are ye when men shall hate you, and when they shall separate you from their company, and reproach you, and *cast out your name as evil*, for the Son of man's sake" (Luke 6:22).

Her Desire to Be Taught

> "I would . . . bring Thee into my mother's house that Thou mightest instruct me; I would cause Thee to drink . . . of the juice of my pomegranate" (8:2, mg.).

If for one moment she thought otherwise, she is now conscious that she is utterly ignorant in herself and that she knows nothing yet as she ought to know. This is the artistry of the "skillful Workman"—to illuminate a soul with His Light, and yet to keep it conscious of its own ignorance—to be "Wisdom" to the redeemed one, yet to keep the earthen vessel from appropriating that wisdom as its own, so that it may ever cry, "Instruct me."

The Shulamite cries, "Teach me—then I would cause Thee to drink, to be refreshed through me, whom Thou hast always compared to a pomegranate" (see 4:3). He is still the center of her whole being; she has lost step, but not Him as her life. Her aim is still that *He* may be satisfied.

The Soul's Cry After Her Resting Place

> "His left hand should be under my head, and His right hand should embrace me" (8:3).

However foolish and ignorant she may be, there is no question as to the integrity of her heart; her will is ever kept immovably set to obey. "I only desire to be taught," she says. "That He may have His way and be satisfied is all I want. Oh for the rest and the upholding of the Everlasting Arms!" Ah, she thought she knew how to keep step, but she sees she is as helpless as ever. She must needs be carried. Now she knows what is meant by being a "little one," and understands the Master's words that the greatest in His Kingdom is as a little child (Matthew 18:4). She is maturing in truth, for she is progressing from "the cross to the cradle"! Her growth in the stature of Christ will be manifested in the child-spirit which evermore lies down in the Father's bosom.

The Soul at Rest and the Well-Beloved's Care

> " I adjure you, O daughters of Jerusalem, Why should ye stir up, or why should ye awaken love, until it please?" (8:4, mg.).

The soul out of touch no sooner cried out for her resting place than she found herself as a babe in the Everlasting Arms! As the mother hears the faintest cry of her little child, so the Well-Beloved responded, "Here I am," to His purchased one (Isaiah 58:9). While she struggled and said, "I would, I, I," He was obliged to wait to be gracious; but her first helpless cry after His heart, and His upholding power, brought her into rest.

When the soul in union with the Lord is conscious of the least cloud, a quiet turning to the Father's heart and a restful dependence upon the blood of sprinkling which ever speaks upon the mercy seat within the veil is the only way into step again. "And if any man sin, we have an Advocate with the Father, Jesus Christ the righteous: and He is the propitiation!" (1 John 2:1–2).

The hidden one at rest will be cared for by her Lord. He speaks again to the daughters of

Jerusalem and bids them leave His redeemed one
to His keeping.

At each stage of the divine life, the "daughters" seem to need His charge. The "sons of the
prophets" came to Elisha at every point where he
took a new step forward in following Elijah—until at last they stood "afar off" to watch the consequences of such a persistent walk. So these "daughters" seem to come to the soul in the Song of Songs.
Possibly they had something to do with her recent
experience and so called forth this renewed charge
from the Lord.

They may have seen her in fresh activity in the
vineyard, beheld her as a Spirit-equipped worker,
and pressed upon her to go here and there—not
knowing that she was still as empty and useless as
she ever had been *when out of His will.* If she lis-
tened to their voices, she would soon go beyond
her measure of grace. However "great the need"
or "important the call," of what use is her going
unless He sends her?

The "daughters" who seek to "stir up" to service other God-possessed souls are a serious source
of danger at every stage of experience. They are
not disposed to keep "hands off" at any time!
Therefore the Well-Beloved asks them *why* they
should seek to stir up the soul that is in *His* hands.
His love that now fills and constrains her will

awaken and impel her forth in the path of His will whensoever He pleases, for He will work in her both to will and to do of His good pleasure (Philippians 2:13, KJV).

Chapter 22

"Leaning on Jesus' bosom one . . . whom Jesus loved" (John 13:23, KJV).

LEANING ON THE BELOVED

"Who is this that cometh up from the wilderness, leaning upon her Beloved?" (8:5).

A pause, and again the daughters of Jerusalem exclaim, "Who is this?" as they behold the hidden one emerging from her time of rest in the Well-Beloved's care. They see her now *leaning* upon her Beloved, for she has learned that she can only keep in step with Him as she leans upon Him every moment in utter dependence and helplessness.

It is possible that in the activity of service, pressed on every hand by the claims of "open doors" or by the gathering in of "precious fruits," she had failed to keep sacred her hours of waiting on her Lord.

In the full assurance of union with Him, and in

the abundance of His life working through her, she may have thought that He would supply her need and renew her strength in the midst of busy service. This He never fails to do when the "claims" are real needs; but warped and unreasonable "claims" come that are not of Him: "souls"—who seek to draw nourishment from the earthen vessel instead of from God Himself; "questions"—from hearts that should learn to trust and not attempt to trace the dealings of God until He pleases to reveal His purposes; "calls"—from Christians who have sought guidance after making their own plans! All these things come to those who faithfully seek to be the "servants of all."

The "hidden one" must learn that the pressure of the needs of others, fancied or real, must never intrude upon the sacred hours of waiting on the Lord. Active service especially demands these times alone with God. The Master needed them, for do we not read: "Great multitudes came together to hear, and to be healed. . . . But He withdrew Himself in the deserts, and prayed" (Luke 5:15–16)?

In the face of all the *real* needs, *He* withdrew! Nay, child of God, it is not waste of time; it is *economy*, for our service is fruitless without the full power of His abundant life, which must be renewed at His feet day by day.

As soon as there is a sense of "pressure," it is all important that we should get alone with God. The "claims" may make this seem impossible, but He can make the way clear *if we know our need* and are willing to retire from the vineyards as soon as we hear His call—leaving His work to Him who is alone responsible, recognizing that *He* is in control.

The Well-Beloved, in His watchful keeping of His loved one, saw that she did not understand her need. So He allured her into the wilderness of rest by hiding Himself for a moment (8:1–3), simply to draw her attention from the vineyards to seek instruction at His feet. We have seen how she regained her resting place, while her Beloved speaks for her to the busy daughters of Jerusalem, forbidding them to stir her up until He pleased.

"Leaning upon her Beloved!"

To bring the soul to entire reliance and dependence upon Him is "the end of the Lord" (James 5:11)—the purpose of His varied dealings, whether in the "valley" or on the "mountaintop."

"Leaning upon her Beloved!" *This* is the outcome of the life of union—what life more simple or more blessed! In this privileged position the hidden one comes forth to renewed service and activity. "Leaning upon her Beloved" to be taught by Him.

The Well-Beloved's Instructions

1. Concerning the earthen vessel

"Under the apple tree I awakened thee" (8:5).

While she leans upon her Beloved, He answers the cry of her heart for instruction in the mysteries of the Kingdom.

He reminds her of her natural condition and of the days when she was first awakened and born into the family of God. She must never—because of His abounding grace toward her—make the mistake of thinking herself to be a *heavenly* vessel. The Treasure of Christ is lodged in a body of fragile clay, that the excellency of the power may manifestly be of God, and not of her.

Moreover, she will need to be kept full of the divine life, if her own peculiar personal characteristics are to be controlled and used by her Lord. It is not enough to know that the Beloved dwells within. She will need, every moment, *as a vessel*, to be kept environed by the Presence of God, "in Him [to] live, and move, and have [her] being" (Acts 17:28), if the shape of the vessel is not to hinder the manifestation of Him who graciously consents to make her a habitation of God by the Spirit.

2. Concerning the jealousy of God

"Set Me as a seal upon thine heart, as a seal upon thine arm:
for love is strong as death, jealousy is hard as the grave; the
flashes thereof are flashes of fire, a most vehement flame.
Many waters cannot quench love, neither can the floods
drown it" (8:6–7, mg.).

The first words are often quoted as spoken by
the bridal soul; but following those of the Well-
Beloved about her natural condition, they have
far more significance if taken as coming from Him.
Seeing her deep, deep need of Him, He cries, "Set
Me as a seal upon thine heart." The "love" that is
"strong as death," and which led Him to the death
of the cross, breaks forth in jealous yearning that
this soul for whom He died should be wholly kept
for Him in heart and hand. His jealousy over His
redeemed one is "hard as the grave." He cannot
overlook one spot or wrinkle in a member of His
Bride; therefore, He will deal with all that is of
earth in her with flashes of fire, so that she may be
as pure gold, and as transparent glass, in the day
when she will be one of those presented to Himself as a sharer of His throne.

The Well-Beloved tells His hidden one that no
flood of trial or sorrow can ever quench His love,
just as no riches can buy it. The jealousy of God
is as "a most vehement flame" over each blood-
bought soul—therefore, constrained with the love

of God, St. Paul said to the Corinthians: "I am jealous over you with a jealousy of God, for I espoused you to one husband, that I might present you as a pure virgin to Christ" (2 Corinthians 11:2, mg.).

Oh child of God, hidden in His heart, abide in this deep love of the eternal God. Listen to His words, "Continue ye in My love" (John 15:9, KJV), and welcome the flashes of fire proceeding from that love, the fire that seeks to purify you as fine gold.

Dwell in the God who is consuming fire; thus shall you see the King in His beauty, and dwell on high!

Chapter 23

"Beloved, if our heart condemn us not, we have boldness toward God; and whatsoever we ask, we receive of Him" (1 John 3:21–22).

COMMUNION WITH THE WELL-BELOVED

"We have a little sister. . . . What shall we do for our sister? . . . We will build upon her . . . battlements of silver, . . . we will enclose her with boards of cedar" (8:8–9, mg.).

Leaning upon her Beloved, what privileges belong to the hidden one! He whispers to her, "If ye abide in Me, and My words abide in you, ask whatsoever ye will, and it shall be done unto you" (John 15:7), and she replies, "We have a little sister . . . what shall we do for our sister?" She may speak to Him freely now about all who are upon her heart, assured that they are upon His heart too.

He replies, "We will build upon her battlements," or "enclose her with boards," as if to say, "She shall be dealt with according to her need; leave her now to Me." It is sufficient to know that when "*He heareth*," "*we have*" the petitions we desire of Him.

Did not Abraham's intercourse with God so hold back the judgment on Sodom that Lot was saved? Abraham himself did not need to go in eager haste to his deliverance; rather, as he "stood before the Lord" the angel messengers were sent.

Thus may the children of God gain admittance to the sanctuary, and in fellowship with a living, all-powerful Lord, place such "battlements" around their loved ones as will guard and keep them unknown to themselves, until, in His fullness of time, they are brought to know the Lord.

Thus will the Well-Beloved teach His hidden ones to use the privilege of their position and learn to move the hand that moves the world, as they stand, in fellowship with Him, in intercession "God-ward for the people."

The King's Business

"Solomon had a vineyard. . . . He let out the vineyard unto keepers. My vineyard, which is mine, is before me. . . . Thou, O Solomon, shalt have the thousand, and those that keep the fruit . . . two hundred" (8:11–12).

The soul, leaning upon her Beloved, finds Him

a skillful teacher. He first had to make her know *herself*, and her position as an earthen vessel; then the jealous love of the God who owned her. Now He turns to the practical affairs of life, that she may learn to be a faithful steward in the smallest detail. The life of union with Him must be manifested in every word, look, and action. She must be permeated with the heavenly spirit, even in that which appears to be of the smallest moment.

The Lord is faithful to all who truly watch for His teaching and leading every moment of the day. "I will instruct thee, and teach thee in the way which thou shalt go" (Psalm 32:8) may be true of the way in the least or in the greatest matter, and souls who are "leaning upon the Beloved" become intuitively sensitive as to what is "worthy of God," and are given increasingly to know the mind of the Lord in the practical actions of daily life. What has been called the "secular" part of life now becomes the "outward business" of the King.

The purchased one is manifestly in the confidence of her Well-Beloved; His interests are hers. She knows that He has other vineyards entrusted to keepers to whom He has said, "Occupy till I come," but she turns to the vineyard entrusted to her, as it lies before her. She is conscious that He must teach her how to be skillful in business, so that He may have His rightful revenues.

It was said of David, after his anointing by the Spirit, that he was "skillful in business" (1 Samuel 16:18, mg.); and Daniel, who had such great visions of God, was no "visionary" in practical life, as we are shown by the fact that his enemies could find no occasion of fault in him in the King's affairs committed to his care.

King Solomon must have his rightful revenues, says His "fellow-worker," but her knowledge of her Lord, and her enlightened judgment as to what is "worthy of God," tells her that she must be generous, as well as just, to those who gather the fruits under her control. She knows that the King would exact no revenue at their cost, for the laborer is worthy of his hire. He must not be dishonored by their being underpaid, or else they, in their turn, will be unable to act worthily of Him.

Moreover, there are eternal consequences attached to her stewardship: if she is to reign with her Lord, she must be taught how to "judge the smallest matters," for "the saints shall judge the world" (1 Corinthians 6:2). She must be trained to apply the laws of the heavenly Kingdom, as set forth in the Sermon on the Mount, to the practical circumstances of her life.

The King as Counselor

" Thou that dwellest in the gardens, the companions hearken for Thy voice; cause me to hear it" (8:13).

The hidden one has learned to walk very silently with her God. The talkative disposition of early days has passed away. She has no desire now to blaze abroad the secrets of His love. The life hidden in the heart of God is a very deep and a very silent one. When God speaks, He speaks with a purpose, and the soul is learning to partake of His divine silence. She cannot talk now for the sake of talking, neither can she listen to, or pass on to her neighbors, the thousand petty trifles that so easily impress those whose minds are set upon earthly things.

The Well-Beloved dwells in the garden of her soul. She tells Him that the companions are eagerly listening for His voice through her; will He please cause her to hear it, so that she may speak only when He speaks! She craves to be but a voice which passes away, leaving the Living Word in the hearts around.

He has promised to be a Wonderful Counselor if she will permit the government of her whole being to remain upon His shoulders. He will cause her to know the way wherein she should walk as she goes forth every moment "leaning upon her Beloved."

The Heart Cry of the Bridal Soul

"Make haste, my Beloved, and be thou like to a gazelle . . . upon the mountains" (8:14, mg.).

She longs for the day of His appearing to the world—for that glorious day when He shall be marveled at in all them that believe; therefore, in unison with the Eternal Spirit, she makes intercession according to the will of God and prays with deep desire: "Make haste, my Beloved," for she is "looking for, and earnestly desiring ["hastening," mg.] the coming of the day of God," and is, according to His promise, looking for "*new* heavens and a *new* earth, wherein dwelleth righteousness" (2 Peter 3:12–13).

Clothed in fine linen, bright and pure, the redeemed ones are then presented to their Lord, with no spot or wrinkle or any such thing (Ephesians 5:27). "Made ready" by Him in the fire, they are clear as crystal, transparent as glass. The body of humiliation has been made like unto the glorious body of the Lord; it is luminous with the light of the Lamb which shines through undimmed.

Even now they are nothing but capacities through which God may manifest His glory.

The glorious destiny of the Bride is to be a tabernacle of God, that He may dwell among men. The nations will walk by the light given through the Bride-city. From the throne of God in the midst thereof will flow a pure river of life, and there shall be crops of fruit (Revelation 22:2, mg.)—ample provision for the healing of the nations—and there shall be no more anything accursed (Revelation 22:3, mg.).

The Bride reigns with her Lord unto the ages of ages.

> All, all in His new creation
>   The glory of God shall see;
> And the lamp for that light eternal
>   The Bride of the Lamb shall be.
>
> A golden lamp in the heavens,
>   That all may see and adore,
> The Lamb who was slain and who liveth,
>   Who liveth for evermore.

•　　•　　•

"GOD [IS] ALL IN ALL"

APPENDIX

Note A

"Is the soul to cease from active service when this revelation comes?" will be the question in many hearts.

Unless under very definite guidance to the contrary, experience says *no,* for the past can be dealt with at the place called Calvary; and in dependence upon the immediate inflow of the life of Jesus, by "faith in the working of God" (Colossians 2:12), the soul can have power to carry on its service from duty, if not with a sense of delight.

However deeply God may be dealing with us, we may always rely upon His energizing power for all that lies in the path of duty if we cast ourselves upon Him. To shrink back because we have lost our "creaturely" delight in service would be giving occasion to the flesh, and yielding to self-pity. That God is dealing with us and revealing our true condition can never be a sufficient reason for refusing to help the souls who come to us in their need.

Moreover, if we are conscious that we are involved in responsibilities laid upon us by *others*, and not by Him, we must commit each difficulty to Him, and in His own time and way He will set us free. He may for the moment use our bonds as the very means for the practical crucifixion of our own life and plans.

Note B

It is very important that the soul should not lose its rest in seeking to know the Lord. "Thou canst go no faster than a full dependence on God can carry thee" (Wm. Law). The Well-Beloved will lead on safely, if we are but true in aim and quick in obedience to every indication of His will.

We must remember at this point the danger of the impetuosity of the creature-life. The Divine Spirit alone can teach true cooperation with His working. We may definitely trust Him not to permit us to lag behind or press beyond His leadings. It is needful that each degree of union should be established before we are led on to the next.

Note C

The question may be asked, "How are we to know when the Lord calls us to arise and follow on?"

By a deep inward cry to know Him better being awakened in our hearts—an unspeakable yearning after God—created by the Divine Spirit. Desire is always God's preparation for a fuller communication of Himself; it is, so to speak, the *vacuum* for Him—the emptiness, that He can fill.

"We which have believed do enter into rest" (Hebrews 4:3, KJV). In the time of repose, resting upon the everlasting arms, let each soul remain there with quiet heart until it hears the voice of the Well-Beloved saying, "Arise and come away."

Note D

It is because the children of God do not apprehend the *two* aspects of crucifixion with Christ that they fail to realize abundant life in practical experience. The *objective* or finished work of Christ in His death and resurrection is the basis of the *subjective* work of the Holy Spirit in us.

Objectively, the death of Christ was not only a propitiation for sin but was, in the purpose of God, the death of all for whom He died.

In our position before God we who are believers are *in Him*, the Cleft Rock—*planted into His death*. The Holy One became a curse for the accursed ones, that the accursed Adam-life might be nailed to the cross with the substitute, the Lamb of God.

Subjectively, it is the work of the Spirit of God to apply to us the power of Christ's death and resurrection; to bring us inwardly into correspondence with our "position" in Christ—crucified, buried, risen, and ascended in the Redeemer.

Both the "objective" and "subjective" aspects must be made real to the soul by the power of the Holy Spirit if "life out of death" is to be known in practical reality.

On our part, if we have been brought by the mercy of God to truly hate ourselves—our "own life" (Luke 14:26) as well as our sins—and to recognize that all is accursed, being heartily willing to renounce all that we ourselves have, we may turn to Calvary and see that in Christ we *are* delivered, being dead to that wherein we were held (Romans 7:6, KJV).

In dependence upon the Divine Spirit, we may appropriate the death of Christ as our death and count upon the immediate inflow of the life of the Risen Lord to possess us to the fullest capacity of the earthen vessel.

From this point—the faith position that we have been crucified with Christ—we may expect the Holy Spirit to bear witness, and "make to die" the "doings of the body" in ever deepening power, while He teaches us increasingly to hate the garment spotted by the flesh and to glory in the cross of the Lord Jesus Christ, through whom the world is crucified to us and we unto the world.

The Eternal Spirit—charged with the work of applying to us Christ's death and communicating the resurrection life of Christ—will cause us always to bear about the dying of Jesus. Thus shall be manifested in our mortal flesh the life also of Jesus, and in the power of that endless life we shall be energized to labor according to *His working*, which will be working in us mightily.

Note E

> "Brethren, be not children in *mind:* howbeit in malice be ye babes, but in mind be men ["of full age," mg.]" (1 Corinthians 14:20).

In the work of renovation, or re-creation, the *mind* must be renewed as well as the heart. The "understanding" must be purged from old ideas, old ways of thinking—the wisdom of the "natural man"* (1 Corinthians 2:14)—as well as his sins. Only thus can the Lord truly put His laws into the mind so that we may be transformed by the "renewing of the mind" to discern the will of God (Romans 12:2).

There is a child stage of the new creation in Christ Jesus, which should develop into the stature of a "full-grown man" (Ephesians 4:13) "ripe in understanding" (1 Corinthians 2:6, CH).

---

* Properly, man considered as endowed with the *anima*, the living principle, as distinguished from the *spiritual* principle (Conybeare's note).

The word "perfect" used by St. Paul denotes this "full-grown man" (according to Conybeare— see his note on Philippians 3:13—"perfect" is the antithesis of "babe"); and to bring every believer into the presence of God "full-grown in Christ" was the desire of Paul's heart and the end for which he labored (Colossians 1:28).

The "full grown" are characterized by the "full assurance of *understanding*" (Colossians 2:2). They are able to know the mind of the Lord, as well as His heart; to enter intelligently into His purposes as full-grown sons—able to know His will so that they pray not only "with the spirit" but "with the understanding also" (1 Corinthians 14:15).

The renewed mind is preeminently—

1. A sound mind

> "God hath not given us the spirit of fear; but of power, and of love, and of a sound mind" (2 Timothy 1:7, KJV).

> "Be ye therefore of sound mind, and be sober unto prayer" (1 Peter 4:7).

The sound mind is one which is no longer controlled by the emotional life but is stayed upon God, enabling the soul to walk by an intelligent faith, calmly, and clearly knowing and doing the right on *principle*, as well as through love.

It no longer places undue importance on "glorious experiences," nor is it entirely guided by "voices," "signs," and "impressions"—because the line between right and wrong becomes increasingly defined to its perception, and it sees and chooses deliberately the path of obedience to God, even when it means great cost to itself.

It needs no argument or incentive, or promise of reward, or stirred up emotions, or weighing of consequences, to persuade it to do the right, but it is governed by an inward principle that proceeds from Him, the scepter of whose Kingdom is a scepter of uprightness.

2. A lowly mind

"Serving the Lord with all lowliness of mind" (Acts 20:19).

The matured soul has lost all delusions about itself! It "soberly" (or "solemnly") recognizes its responsibility to cooperate with God up to its "measure of faith" (Romans 12:3).

There is a shrinking back that keeps the soul from fullest cooperation with God. It must know its calling so that in all lowliness of mind it may be what God has ordained it to be in the Body of Christ.

The Apostle Paul said he knew the limit which God had apportioned to him. He had not stretched beyond his limit in going with the gospel to the Corinthians. He knew his "measure" and the extent of the stewardship of grace entrusted to him.

(See 2 Corinthians 10:12–17.)

A matured soul, taught of the Spirit, will know how to use the "measuring rod" so that it may not go beyond its limit (2 Corinthians 10:13, mg.). Serving the Lord in all humility of mind, it will not be "puffed up" because its calling may be that of an "eye" in the body of Christ, or cast down because its place may be the "feet." (See 1 Corinthians 12:15–27.)

In deep humility it will do "nothing through vainglory" but in lowliness of mind will esteem others better than itself—for it will see what *is* better in others, and be so unconscious of itself that comparison will not enter into its thoughts.

3. A spiritual mind

" To be spiritually minded is life and peace" (Romans 8:6, KJV).

In Hebrews 5 we are told that babes are unskillful in the word of righteousness because they are only able to take milk, and not solid food.

The "wisdom of God" can only be spoken among the "full grown" (1 Corinthians 2:6, mg.)—those whom St. Paul describes as "spiritual."

Speaking not "in words which man's wisdom teacheth," he interpreted *spiritual* things to *spiritual* men (1 Corinthians 2:13, mg.), knowing that the natural man could not comprehend the teaching of God's Spirit. (See the entire passage: 1

Corinthians 2:1–16.)

Enlightened by the indwelling Spirit and daily renewed with the divine life, the powers of the renovated mind can be greatly increased.

It can be brought into order and freed from unnecessary or slothful action: its *rapidity* can be quickened, its power of concentration deepened, its accuracy and retention perfected. Its mental detachment can be marvelously increased to see readily the point of view of others who are also taught of God. It is, so to speak, detached from its own experience in ministering to others, and is able to give them the "milk" or the "meat" according to their need. It is like the man who is instructed unto the Kingdom of heaven (Matthew 13:52, KJV), able to bring out of his "treasure" things new and old.

Lastly, the truly spiritual mind has "understanding" that the divine life, manifested through an earthen vessel, must be given room for development and will be manifested according to the shape of the vessel; it is therefore free from all prejudice, partiality, and preconceived ideas of God's working. Thus the soul is able to "see God" in others, and has a "ready mind" (Acts 17:11) to perceive indications of His will and of His working where others can find no trace.

Note F

How can this brief passage in the history of the purchased one be said to describe fellowship with Christ in His sufferings, when it appears as if all had come upon her because she did not respond quickly to her Well-Beloved's call?

We have seen that her hesitation was not a refusal in the *will* but only a shrinking from the pathway of suffering, and we are given but a glimpse into one aspect of what fellowship with Christ means.

Her "sharing the likeness" of His death is faintly seen in the anguish of her soul at the hiding of the face of her Well-Beloved; in her desolation of spirit as she found no comforters; in the hour and power of darkness as the enemy swept upon her like a flood with bitter mocking about the faithfulness of her Lord.

The "shadow" of His cross has come upon her, but only a shadow—a "*likeness*"—for He removed the sting from death as He trod the winepress alone, drank the bitter cup to its dregs, and made propitiation for the sins of the people.

Nought but a "shadow" of death for His redeemed ones—that they might give Him the fellowship He seeks and be conformed to the image of the Lamb.

Note G

It is important that we should know how to deal with God, and "prove the things that differ."

Is it the silence of love which tests the soul to mature its faith; or the silence of grief over some step out of His will? Such must be the heart-searching question when the Lord ceases to speak.

The soul in such a case should cast itself at once at the feet of the Well-Beloved and seek to know His mind. It may always "draw near . . . in full assurance of faith," through the sprinkled blood evermore speaking to God upon the Mercy Seat. It is *always* "accepted in the Beloved."

Sheltering under the blood, the soul should definitely deal with God, renew its abandonment, and with the simplicity of a little child commit its way unto the Lord, trusting Him to reveal and remove the cause of His grief, or—if His silence is the silence of testing—to keep it safely in the path of His blessed will. Having thus rolled our "way upon the Lord," we may rest and wait patiently for Him.

This book was produced by CLC Publications. We hope it has been helpful to you in living the Christian life. CLC is a literature mission with ministry in over 50 countries worldwide. If you would like to know more about us, or are interested in opportunities to serve with a faith mission, we invite you to write to:

CLC Publications
P.O. Box 1449
Fort Washington, PA 19034